WOODWORKER'S GUIDE TO
SELECTING
—— AND ——
MILLING
WOOD

WOODWORKER'S GUIDE TO
SELECTING
— AND —
MILLING
WOOD

CHARLES SELF

BETTERWAY BOOKS

Cincinnati, Ohio

Disclaimer

To prevent accidents, keep safety in mind while you work. Use the safety guards installed on power equipment; they are for your protection. When working on power equipment, keep fingers away from saw blades, wear safety goggles to prevent injuries from flying wood chips and sawdust, wear headphones to protect your hearing, and consider installing a dust vacuum to reduce the amount of airborne sawdust in your woodshop. Don't wear loose clothing, such as neckties or shirts with loose sleeves, or jewelry, such as rings, necklaces or bracelets, when working on power equipment, and tie back long hair to prevent it from getting caught in your equipment.

Woodworker's Guide to Selecting and Milling Wood. Copyright © 1994 by Charles R. Self. Printed and bound in the United States of America. All rights reserved. No part of this book may be reproduced in any form or by any electronic or mechanical means including information storage and retrieval systems without permission in writing from the publisher, except by a reviewer, who may quote brief passages in a review. Published by Betterway Books, an imprint of F&W Publications, Inc., 1507 Dana Avenue, Cincinnati, Ohio 45207. 1-800-289-0963. First edition.

This hardcover edition of *Woodworker's Guide to Selecting and Milling Wood* features a "self-jacket" that eliminates the need for a separate dust jacket. It provides sturdy protection for your book while it saves paper, trees and energy.

98 97 96 95 94   5 4 3 2 1

Library of Congress Cataloging-in-Publication Data

Self, Charles R.
    Woodworker's guide to selecting and milling wood / by Charles R. Self — 1st ed.
        p. cm.
        Includes index.
        ISBN 1-55870-339-X
        1. Woodwork.   2. Wood.   I. Title.
TT180.S39797 1994
684'.08 — dc20   94-19187
                                          CIP

Edited by R. Adam Blake
Cover and interior design by Brian Roeth

Quantity Discounts Available
This and other Betterway Books are available at a discount when purchased in bulk. Schools, organizations, corporations and others interested in purchasing bulk quantities of this book should contact the Special Sales Department of F&W Publications at 1-800-289-0963 (8 A.M.-5 P.M. Eastern Time) or write to this department at 1507 Dana Avenue, Cincinnati, Ohio 45207.

METRIC CONVERSION CHART		
TO CONVERT	**TO**	**MULTIPLY BY**
Inches	Centimeters	2.54
Centimeters	Inches	0.4
Feet	Centimeters	30.5
Centimeters	Feet	0.03
Yards	Meters	0.9
Meters	Yards	1.1
Sq. Inches	Sq. Centimeters	6.45
Sq. Centimeters	Sq. Inches	0.16
Sq. Feet	Sq. Meters	0.09
Sq. Meters	Sq. Feet	10.8
Sq. Yards	Sq. Meters	0.8
Sq. Meters	Sq. Yards	1.2
Pounds	Kilograms	0.45
Kilograms	Pounds	2.2
Ounces	Grams	28.4
Grams	Ounces	0.04

Dedication

To my sister, Donna S. Nowland, with love

About the Author

Charles Self is the author of more than thirty books, many on aspects of woodworking, including *Woodworker's Source Book*, *101 Quick & Easy Woodworking Projects*, *Joinery: Methods of Fastening Wood* and *Working With Plywood*. He has more than nine hundred magazine articles to his credit, for such magazines as *The Family Handyman*, *Popular Science*, *Workbench* and *The Homeowner*. A member of the National Association of Home and Workshop Writers, he has served as consultant/copywriter for a number of major manufacturers. He lives in Bedford, Virginia.

Table of Contents

Foreword

As it is with all books, help is essential to arriving at a finished product, and often is essential in getting a half-decent start. For much of the information on wood, I've worked with my own experience, and that of Bobby Weaver, a good friend who is also a woodworker. For further help on woods, I looked to the American Plywood Association, the California Redwood Association, Georgia-Pacific, Groff & Hearne, Southern Forest Products Association, Woodcraft and The Woodworkers' Store. For information and assistance with tools and tool use, I got much needed help from AMT, Black & Decker (including their DeWalt division), Delta Machinery, Leichtung, Makita, Meisel Hardware, Ryobi America, Sears, Roebuck & Co., Skil and Stanley Tools.

My wife, Frances, managed to keep our world's problems at bay long enough for me to complete the book, and for that, and many other things, I thank her hugely.

Introduction

All kinds of people start working with wood for a great many reasons: We may desire a new bookshelf or stereo component rack, or any of a number of other products that we cannot afford or find in local furniture stores. Or we may feel a need for a kind of furniture that isn't available with any regularity, if at all. Or we may simply want to do something with our hands, and minds, to counteract the factory-made parts of our lives.

Some of us may already have a love for working with wood and working with our hands before beginning the hobby. And some of us may not.

In my case, I had lots of trouble as a kid in shop class: My sanded edges were always rounded when they weren't supposed to be, and I made grooves in flat surfaces while preparing for finishing. I liked wood, and came to love it, but was more than moderately inept at forming it until well after I went to work at Katonah Altar Factory as an all-round helper (the kid who swept up the sawdust and was general gofer, whether for coffee or shaper cutters).

My problems were reduced after I discovered such joys as sanding

Yellow pine, from southern forests.
Courtesy of Southern Forest Products Association.

Timber roads provide needed forest access for logging.
Courtesy of Southern Forest Products Association.

sawdust, which were then hauled off in semis. I guess I was the dust collection system in those days.

Like most kids of my era, I preferred cars and motorcycles to anything else, except—possibly—girls. As soon as I was able to find a job working with cars, I was out of the altar factory, and helping pump gas, build Olds-engined '35 Chevy coupés, rebuild old Harley-Davidson suicide clutch 45s and a Norton Manx 500 thumper, and working at similar nonwoodworking pursuits.

I became a competent shade-tree mechanic long before I gained real competence in woodworking, going to one side of my heritage—my father was an auto mechanic, and one of the best (I am told) for his time and place. After military time, and into college, I returned to woodworking, as a need. College students then couldn't afford enough bookshelves, and probably still can't.

But I scraped up $11.00 for clear pine, stain and Masonite hardboard to build an 84-inch-tall by 36-inch-wide bookshelf. And I borrowed a saw, hammer, push drill, square and folding rule with which to build it.

I don't expect to ever again come close to those prices for pine today, but I'm still building bookshelves. The price of wood has climbed to the point where $.09 a board foot pine is now about $2.25, if you can find it. In Virginia, where I live, white pine is a shipped-in species, and finding clear pine in 1 × 12 is impossible. I can find the top grade, Firsts and Seconds (FAS) 1 × 12 walnut, oak, poplar and a number of other woods, but not clear pine.

The reasons for the increase in price are many, and only partly based on inflationary factors over the years. Little white or sugar pine is

blocks, properly set up radial arm and table saws and similar tools. The foreman, and this recollection is going back to my high school days so it may not be exact, was named John Leather. He was willing to take a little time to help a bumbling, shy kid. Not a lot—he was, after all, busy—

but that little was more than any high school shop teacher had cared enough to provide.

I began to get an inkling of the joy of building things of wood, but couldn't do much at the factory: Most of my duties consisted of filling large burlap sacks with chips and grown in this area of the South. Or, as far as I know, any of the South. Most of the white pine we get comes from Oregon, Maine and British Columbia, so a huge transportation bill is added to the basic cost.

Oak, walnut, poplar, cherry and *yellow* pine are local species that are abundant, and cheap, if you are able to set some aside and let it air dry, and then can take the time to plane it to size.

Like many products, rough, wet wood is cheaper than dried, finish-planed wood. Your labor, a relatively low-cost planer and jointer, and a short ton of time can translate to savings of more than 50 percent on woods such as walnut and cherry. Buy rough from a mill, stack properly and cover the top, and later plane it and joint it, and you're ready to go: Walnut, in its FAS incarnation can cost upwards of $4.50 a board foot today, but I last bought rough walnut for under a quarter of that price.

The process isn't nearly that simple, of course. The walnut didn't automatically convert to $4.50 lumber just by sitting in my yard for a year. First, there's the shrinkage loss while drying, which may amount to as much as 10 percent overall. Then there's the planing loss, at least another 10 percent. Then there's the trimming loss. And, finally, not all the wood even comes close to FAS grading. Some has rot, wormholes, knots or other problems.

But the overall 450 board feet I paid for actually measured about 485 board feet before drying. I got a total of about 350 board feet of planed lumber (or will have, when it's all planed and ready). Of that, about a third or a shade more is FAS, which is a very good figure for a random

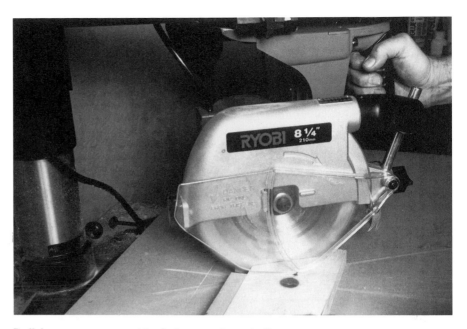

Radial arm saws are great for fast or complex cut-offs.

tree. A quarter would have been more usual.

I paid $360 for the walnut. The FAS alone is worth about $525. At a rough guess, I saved enough to pay for a $400 lightweight planer with that one batch.

The figures are deceiving, of course. You must have storage space for the wood. You must also have a planer and jointer, a table saw, and, with luck, a radial arm saw—or know someone who does, and who will allow you to use them. You must pay for the electricity you use, and you're going to have a better than fair amount of sweat equity, and splinter removal time, in the job.

On a cheap-shot basis, you can slip by with just a jointer, leaving the planer for later. Jointers flatten wood well, and usually are used only for edging boards—jointing. But they also plane and, in fact, do a better job of removing cupping (the curling up of board edges) than do most planers. You're more limited in width, because most home shop jointers are 6-inch-cut models, but

most of us also work more with lumber under 6 inches wide than we do with lumber out to 12 inches wide.

This, though, is the ultimate form of saving money when buying wood for projects. There are steps up to, and actually one past, the above that are described in this book. The investment in space and tools doesn't have to be large to allow reasonable savings in project materials. Add a 6-inch jointer to your shop, and you will spend less than $400, sometimes far less. And you may find a good used one. My friend Bobby Weaver, who is in several photos throughout this book and many of my others, outfitted his shop entirely with used tools at first, and is now replacing them, fairly slowly, with new tools, where he feels it is necessary. (The jointer is one area where he feels the need, for the used one he bought many years ago is balky at times and also lacks a safety guard.)

You need to know a good deal about wood to make informed choices for your projects: It's fine to look at a plan and note that the designer says to use cherry — or some other wood. But what if you prefer to use redwood? Is it going to be suitable in strength, workability and accepting finish? If it misses suitability in one area, can that be compensated for if enough other requirements are fulfilled? Can you use pine and save much money over cherry? What will the appearance be like? How will that work, take stain, and generally finish out compared to cherry?

Those are just a few of the questions I've answered in this book. You will also find details on different planers, jointers and other tools that are essential to the wood preparation process. And there's plenty of information on drying wood, with and without your own kiln.

The idea is to make you a better-informed user of wood in your projects, reducing costs, adding pleasure, and, often, making the work easier. If, like me, you change every project designed by someone else, and often design your own, then a solid knowledge of woods and how they differ from each other (as well as how they're alike, overall) can make your changes, and your original designs, far better. As an example, about eighteen months before writing this, I built two bookcases of clear redwood. Redwood is not often used for such work, and is fairly weak in thin cross sections, but for bookcases particularly that is easily converted to a plus. Use a contrasting wood, ¾ inch thick and ½ inch deep, glued into a ¾-inch-wide × ⅜-inch-deep groove down the center of the shelf bottoms. I used pine. The white contrasts nicely with the red, so I stained neither wood, and laid on a multiple coating of ZAR Flat Polyurethane — six coats. Redwood is soft and scratches easily, so a good, durable

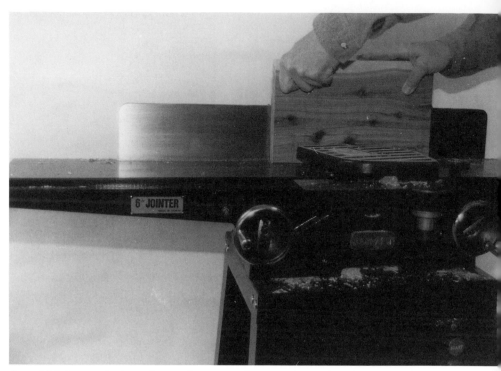

A good jointer may be lower in actual cost now than ever before: This AMT needs some assembly on arrival, but is a real money saver and presents you with a long bed, making work on longer boards and projects easier.

polyurethane finish is essential.

As another example, I recently built myself a new computer desk, using a combination of red and white oak. As usual, I regretted the red oak after starting, but had it on hand and mostly glued up. Part of the problem was using red oak plywood, plus white oak and red oak and some ash solid wood. Still, the entire unit has a really acceptable appearance because wood pores were filled with Behlen's Pore O Pac. The color is consistent throughout, as is the finish coating, though finishing qualities and color of red and white oak differ considerably. But it was much extra work, and if circumstances had been different, I would have gone with white oak alone.

I knew in advance I'd volunteered for hard labor, because I knew the woods. Being surprised by the extra work would have really taken the fun out of the project.

And that's what this book is all about: having fun with your projects, and not being surprised by extra work — at least, not being surprised by extra work caused by the woods used. Fun is measured in money spent versus time entertained, I believe, and keeping the first part low helps a lot in making the entire equation work, at least for most people. Thus, we cover ways of getting woodworking-quality woods at lowest cost, while extending our capabilities in working with those woods, because knowing any wood is a large step towards using that wood properly and well, whether we're working with solid woods, manufactured woods such as plywoods, or treated woods.

Woodworker's Guide to Selecting and Milling Wood is aimed at saving you money on materials, and not breaking your back with work, though there's plenty of detail to let you work from the ground up if you want to. You'll find every type of woodworker's wood covered, from solid woods of many kinds, to hardwood and softwood plywoods, to so-called engineered woods, and on to pressure-treated (PT) woods. The use of pressure-treated wood isn't a high priority for a great many woodworkers, but PT wood offers some help, and some challenges, in a couple of areas, so it is worthwhile to cover the material, at least briefly.

Plywood is covered because it is a heavily used material today, and knowing the grades and how to spec them can result in a major cost saving in larger projects, and a major time saving in smaller projects.

I hope you enjoy this book as much as I've enjoyed writing it, with the able urging of my editor, Adam Blake, and with some of his very valuable help, too.

Redwood is usually used as outdoor material: This wren house is one example of that use.

PART ONE

IDENTIFYING WOOD

Chapter One

THE STRUCTURE OF WOOD

Wood exemplifies the natural beauty of the world around us. Although man may change wood forms and finishes, the mere existence of its grain and sheer beauty of the color and texture of the wood reminds us of its natural state. Wood is many things, so many it is hard to imagine, but for the woodworker, wood is the absolute and ultimate construction material for projects ranging from the size of a pea, on up past the size of a house. Wood is the natural resource that mankind has used longer than any other, except probably stone. And life was a lot more comfortable after wood and stone were combined to work as tools and housing and to fill other needs.

Most of us who have worked with wood over a number of years prefer it to all other construction materials, whether for building erection, or smaller projects, such as boxes, barrels, furniture of many kinds and types, toys, shelves . . . well, you name it. Whatever it is, at one time or another, it has probably been built of wood—and may still be, somewhere, somehow.

Think of the old wooden bodies on station wagons: Those are no longer built (and someone will have to explain to me why companies

All woods start their journeys into our homes and shops in the forests of the world.
Courtesy of Southern Forest Products Association.

Even conifers have green leaves, though we call them needles.
Courtesy of Southern Forest Products Association.

print wood patterns on metal and plastic and slap them onto vehicles: The stuff doesn't begin to appear wood-like). But you can get them reconstructed at a number of places, so it will probably be another hundred years before they're in danger of disappearing from the roads. And that will be from wear and tear on metal parts.

Wood provides almost the ideal project construction material: Tools readily shape it, dampness (especially with heat) helps it bend, and abrasion, as well as other stresses, grind it down only slowly. No synthetic material equals wood for working qualities and finished appearance, especially if we keep in mind the needs of the wood when making projects.

For larger projects needing wide, flat expanses of wood, plywood is helpful because it tends to equalize expansion and contraction rates in different directions, reducing splits and warping and cupping. Solid woods are ideal for areas such as cabinet or storage project door frames where narrower stock isn't as subject to extremes of expansion and contraction and the resulting problems.

How does wood get to the point where we find it such a fine material with which to work?

PHOTOSYNTHESIS

The process known as photosynthesis accounts for the growth of trees, as with all other green plants. Energy from sunlight in a complex chemical reaction joins with water from the ground to form sugars, all taking place with the help of chlorophyll, the substance that gives green leaves their color.

I'm not going to go over the entire journey of wood growth, but here's a brief explanation. Carbon dioxide passes into leaves through the stomata to join water rising from root hairs—where the water enters by osmosis. Water, or sap, flows through the sapwood to the tree's crown. The sapwood is the living wood in a tree, and serves two purposes, aided in some cases by the heartwood that no longer transfers sap: Wood provides the strength to keep a tree standing; it also stores the food created by the leaves. The inner bark is the transfer agent for the food created in the leaves, which is the reason girdling a tree—removing the bark layers down to the sapwood—inevitably kills a tree. New wood is produced in the cambium, which encloses the living parts of the tree trunk, or bole. Wood shows growth rings in those parts of the world where seasonal growth *stops* for part of the year. In tropical areas where seasonal changes don't stop growth, there are no growth rings in the trees. When sapwood is too far removed from the cambium to serve as a sap flow agent, chemical changes occur, changing its makeup and, often, wood color. Heartwood is thus formed.

Again, it isn't the purpose of this book to do a full treatise on wood growth through all conditions and in all areas. Suffice to say that, once heartwood starts to form, a tree is reaching for maturity. It may have decades, even centuries, to go, and there are all sorts of failures along the way, but tree growth continues as outlined above.

TREE CELL STRUCTURE

Different cell structures in the tree create different handling needs for particular parts of a tree, and for particular trees. This is an incredibly complex subject, and I am going to attempt to simplify it, without losing too much meaning, because the different characteristics of hardwoods and softwoods, as well as the different characteristics of different kinds of hardwoods, are strongly based on these cell structure types.

First, let's define softwoods and hardwoods. The actual definitions are simpler than we might expect, but have nothing to do with hardness or softness. Cone-bearing trees, or conifers, that do not drop their needles (leaves) are generally classed as *softwoods*. A few are deciduous—leaf dropping—but by far the greatest number are not. These are the gymnosperms, which is the plant grouping that has naked seeds. *Hardwoods* come from broad-leafed trees, usually deciduous, but not always (the live oak is an example of an evergreen hardwood, and its wood is very hard), with protected seeds, or angiosperms. Note that the definitions actually have nothing to do with softness or hardness. As a rule, softwoods are less strong than hardwoods, less dense and lighter. But balsa is a hardwood, as is tulip poplar in the domestic varieties, and both are far softer than the trees classed as southern pine, and are far less strong, and far lighter—in the case of balsa, it is the lightest commercially available wood.

The different *figures*—not grain, but figure is what you usually see when viewing a board—we look for and use for woodworking purposes come from differing cell arrangements. Those cell arrangements are determined by type of wood and species of tree, but they serve the purposes already covered—food transmittal and mechanical support.

SOFTWOOD STRUCTURE

Softwood structure is considerably easier to deal with than hardwood structure, so we'll take it first.

The primary softwood cell is called a *tracheid*, and is a long, hairlike structure, usually some hundred times as long as it is wide. The various species have different length tracheids, but an average cubic inch of softwood may contain some four

This cross section of a Ponderosa pine shows growth rings. The light bands are earlywood. Dark bands are latewood. Paired light and dark bands equal a year's growth.

million of these cells. Texture in softwood is based on the diameter of the tracheids, with redwood having the largest, and, thus, the coarsest texture. Fine-textured woods have smaller diameter tracheids, often as small as one-third the diameter of the redwood (measured in microns: For those who care, the range is from twenty to sixty). There is a difference, in the same tree, in diameter of tracheids in earlywood and latewood. Earlywood is also known as springwood, and latewood is sometimes termed summerwood. Earlywood, thus, is growth early in the year, while latewood is growth later in the year, closing up the growing season. The earlywood may be larger in diameter, and the cell walls may be thinner. The variation from earlywood to latewood determines the evenness of the grain: In the southern pines, the difference is extreme, often as much as triple, while in other woods there is very little variation. Problems occur if this difference in density is not taken into account—earlywood wears away at a faster rate (such as during sanding,

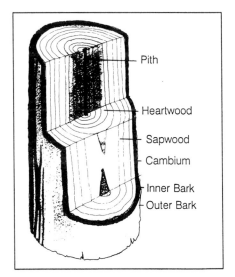

Cross section of a tree.

after the project is finished and in use, and so on).

Many softwood, or coniferous, species also have resin canals; these trees are lined with living cells that ooze resin into the canals. In North America these canals normally are found in pines, spruces, larches and Douglas firs. Our hardwoods don't have them—but some exotic species do. Resin canals in pines are often large enough to be seen with the naked eye.

Obviously, or maybe not so obviously, the resins in these canals can create problems. Sapwood resin canals contain liquid resin, which may eventually work its way to the surface if not set adequately during drying. Setting takes a temperature in the kiln of at least 175°, so air drying simply doesn't do much good with such woods, a point to keep in mind when home-drying softwoods. You must at least finish softwood in a kiln with the correct temperature: Whether you can do so in a solar kiln or not is problematical. I'd say it isn't worth taking a chance if you're working up wood for projects of importance. Air dry to 15 to 18 percent moisture content, and then let a commercial kiln finish the wood for you for best results. For even better, and cheaper, results, avoid softwoods in the four species with resin canals, all in the *Pinaceae* family. Thus, don't use *Pinus, Picea, Larix* or *Pseudotsuga* for projects where bleedthrough of resins might create a problem.

Softwood rays (longitudinal stripes that run at right angles to a tree's axis) are usually a single cell wide, but may be forty times as long, and are just about invisible without a microscope. Thus, there is no noticeable ray figure, or pattern, on quartersawn lumber.

HARDWOOD STRUCTURE

Now that I've oversimplified softwood structure to a fare-thee-well, it's time to do the same for hardwoods. And here there's a real problem, for hardwood structures as shown in their cell types are far more varied than softwood structures. There are several differences between North American hardwoods and softwoods. North American hardwoods lack resin canals. Some

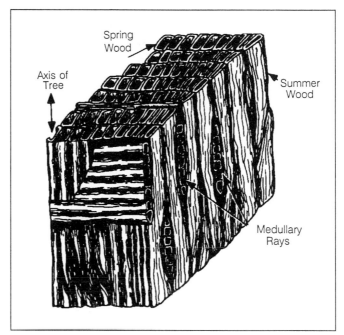

Structure of wood.

tropical exotics contain gum ducts. Rays in hardwoods are the most obvious difference in many cases, especially in oaks where quartersawing produces a pronounced, and lovely, ray pattern. (As noted, softwood rays are invisible until one slaps a microscope on the wood.) To keep this explanation as short as possible, we'll look at the sap-conducting cells for hardwood, which are called *vessel elements.* They are of large diameter, have thin cell walls and no end walls. They're arranged in the tree in an end-to-end pattern, thus forming a canal for sap. The smallest, thickest cells in a hardwood tree are the fibers, which have closed ends and thick walls. These provide strength.

When vessels are cut across their ends, they form pores, so that hardwoods are also classed as porous woods (softwoods, by contrast, are nonporous). Some hardwoods are listed as diffuse porous, and others as ring porous. Both sound more complex than they really are: Ring porous woods have the pores arranged in concentration in the earlywood; diffuse porous woods have pores ar-

ranged fairly evenly throughout, forming a smoother wood. Oaks are ring porous woods, with their characteristic roughness. Cherry is a diffuse porous wood, as is maple, birch, basswood and tulip poplar. And there are groups of woods that fall between the two extremes, forming semi-ring porous woods (or semi-diffuse porous woods, the term depending on the writer, the mood, and the phase of the moon). The *Juglans* family, including black walnut and butternut, is an inhabitant of this category.

Pore size is also used as a gauge of texture, with oak being a rough-textured wood and cherry, maple and other smaller pored woods being smooth textured.

Tyloses are another type of structure that forms in some hardwoods. Tyloses are sac-like structures that appear in the cavities between vessel elements. Some species have many of them, as in white oak, and others, such as red oak and hickory, have very few. Tyloses obstruct the flow of air or liquids through wood, making those species packed with them much better for making barrels, boats and so on.

To further complicate this explanation of hardwood structure, there are other longitudinal cells to go with fibers, though none can be seen individually. Masses are easily distinguished from surrounding cells, with fibers usually showing up darker, while two other types, tracheid and parenchyma cells, show up lighter. This information is of real value to the woodworker only when microscopic identification of wood is needed, and these cells will be covered no further here as individual entities, but it is these three types of cells that make up hardwood rays.

Small rays may be only a single cell wide, but others may be forty cells wide and very long (white oak rays to four inches in length are uncommon, but sometimes present). Rays are planes of structural weakness, and checks may form along their planes. They also provide a natural plane for splitting woods, as in shingle-making with a froe and mallet. Getting a smooth surface with rays can get to be work—though it's possible, and the result is lovely. The larger the rays, the larger the problem—chip tear-out relates to ray size. When planing wood with rays, work a bit across the grain, instead of dead-on the grain, and you'll get less tear-out. It is also advisable to make sure all planer knives are freshly sharpened and cleanly honed.

FIGURE

Not as in "Go figure" but as in "Sheest, that wood has a lovely grain." No, it doesn't. It has a lovely *figure*. To save the confusion that so often results from comparing grain, figure and other wood features, and then explaining the way each is

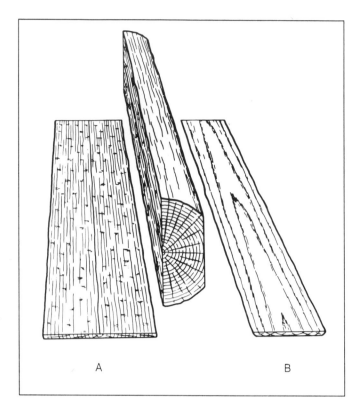

Quartersawn (A) and plainsawn (B) boards.

formed, suffice it to say that figure is the term used to refer to longitudinal markings of wood. That is, the appearance of a board, viewed flat. There are far more complex explanations of what it is, and how it got that way, but figure is a flat look at the wood as it was cut—and it may well be cut in a number of ways, as we know.

In flat sawing, or sawing around the board, the log is flipped after several passes to cut another side, and then is flipped again and so on. Through sawing is also flat sawing, and produces similar patterns in flat-figure boards, for the most part, though there's also a combination of patterns in some of the boards.

Quartersawing is most desirable from a figure, and wood stability, standpoint most of the time, but . . . as always, you must give up something. It is the most wasteful of both time and materials, though you'd never know that from many illustra-

tions. It takes longer, and there are a goodly number of small sawmill operators who don't know how to quartersaw (though few who will admit not knowing), and even more who don't wish to be bothered unless heavily reimbursed. Most noncustom milled wood today is flat sawn. Flat-sawn boards have the characteristic U or V shapes at the board ends.

When wood is cut for plywood, the choices expand even more. Most plywood today is not from sawn logs, but from peeled or sliced logs. Rotary cut, or peeled, logs are mounted on a huge lathe and turned against a very, very sharp blade. This is the usual type of veneer cutting, and is used, according to Georgia-Pacific, in 80 to 90 percent of all veneers. It produces a very bold figure because it follows the log's growth rings.

Plain, or flat-sliced, veneers start with half a log mounted with the heartwood side flat to the carriage.

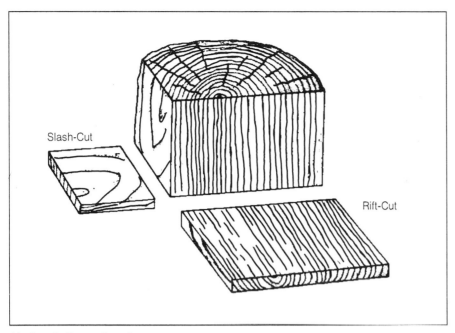

Slash and riftsawn boards.

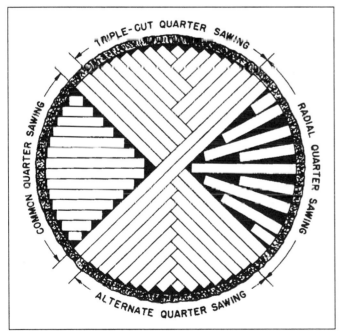

Four methods of quartersawing.

The knife then slices off wood on a line parallel to the guide plate, and gives a figure very much like that of flat-sawn lumber.

Half-round slicing sees the log mounted off-center in the lathe, which gives a cut slightly across the growth rings, to combine the figure of rotary and flat-sliced veneers. This cut is often used on both red and white oaks.

Rift cutting is used primarily on oaks, and mostly on white oaks at that. The rays mentioned earlier radiate from the center of the log something like curved spokes in a wheel, and the rift cut goes perpendicular to these rays to give what is called a comb grain effect. It should be called a comb figure effect, but we're not about to change the world with one short book on wood.

When we combine the effects of different kinds of cutting with the immense number of variations in wood figures themselves, it's readily apparent that the diversity is immense. Within the characteristic appearances of each species, or family, of woods, there are probably an infinite number of variations on the original theme.

And more specialized cutting can change even those! Cone cutting is similar to sharpening a pencil, and can produce a particularly different figure, while cutting tree crotches and burls results in a further amazing variety.

There are bird's-eye figures in maple, flame figures in birch, quilted figures in maple, striped figures in woods with interlocked grain (sweet gums and some elms, among other North American hardwoods), fiddle back figures in mahoganies and other woods, and onward and ever different figures in burls and crotches.

KNOTTY WOOD

Irregularities in wood, other than figure, create problems. Knots are probably the primary problem we all face in finding the wood we want, in both appearance and strength, for a variety of projects, but there are other things that can drive us crazy—sap stain and its blue mess, warp and wane, and checking, among others.

There are times when you will be able to use most defects to reduce the cost of wood. Or you may be able to use them to enhance the appearance of a project. That does include some types of knots, though not nearly all, and it is truly infrequently the case. Mostly, we work around knots and other defects.

Commercial hardwood is graded as if every knot is a defect, which, for

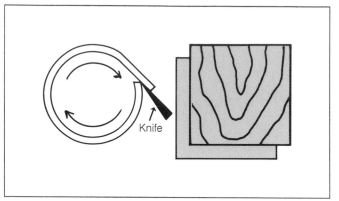

ROTARY

The log is mounted centrally in the lathe and turned against a razor sharp blade, like unwinding a roll of paper. Since the cut follows the log's annular growth rings, a bold variegated grain marking is produced. Eighty to ninety percent of all veneer is cut by the rotary lathe method.

Courtesy of Georgia-Pacific Corporation.

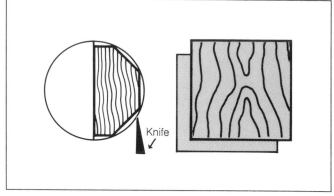

PLAIN OR FLAT-SLICED

The half log, or flitch, is mounted with the heart side flat against the guide plate of the slicer and slicing is done parallel to a line through the center of the log. This produces a variegated figure that is similar to sawn lumber.

Courtesy of Georgia-Pacific Corporation.

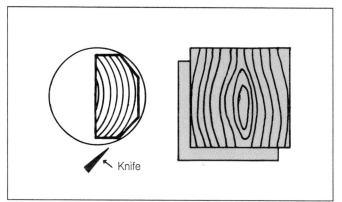

HALF-ROUND SLICING

A method of cutting in which log segments are mounted off-center in the lathe. This results in a cut slightly across the annual growth rings, and visually shows modified characteristics of both rotary and plain sliced veneers. This method of cutting is often used on red and white oak.

Courtesy of Georgia-Pacific Corporation.

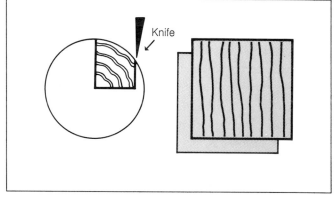

RIFT CUT

Rift cut veneer is produced in the various species of oak. Oak has medullary ray cells which radiate from the center of the log like the curved spokes of a wheel. The rift or comb grain effect is obtained by cutting perpendicularly to these medullary rays either on the lathe or slicer.

Courtesy of Georgia-Pacific Corporation.

small, tight knots, pin knots and some spike knots, may be to your advantage. To start, a knot is nothing more than a part of a limb that got embedded in the tree when the base of a branch became enveloped by the growing trunk. Going into the entire growth process isn't essential, but eventually the surrounded material forms a tight knot and, if there are years of growth added to the first stub, the knot is encased. This be-comes a loose knot, a defect even less desirable. Knotholes crop up when loose knots drop out of the board. Spike knots are formed by the way a board is cut—they are knots that extend across the face of a board and they're usually found only in boards that are created by radial sawing. Flat sawing produces round knots from the same defect. Pin knots crop up in many places. They are smaller than a quarter inch in diameter, and seem to me to always come in groups of three or more.

REACTION WOOD

Reaction wood is *compression* (softwoods) or *tension* (hardwoods) wood, wood formed because a tree does not grow erect—that is, straight up, or near plumb. Leaning trees create wood that presents problems for woodworkers—and for carpenters.

Reaction wood in conifers is

called compression wood because the lower side of the leaning trunk is put under compression. It can be checked by eye: The reaction side of a log has a growth ring that is wider than the rest of the ring, with the heartwood offset towards the upper side. Compression wood problems include lessened wood density, thus lower strength because of a lowered cellulose level. The wood becomes harder and more brittle. It doesn't accept stain as evenly, and may well turn a nail, or split, where regular wood won't. Breakage tends to be sudden and extreme, at lower than normal loadings. It also shrinks more in length — longitudinal shrinkage — a direction that is usually ignored in most domestic woods when figuring shrinkage problems. Too, drying creates uneven stresses, which result in excessive warping — sooner or later, you'll rip a board, doing everything by the book, and note that as the pieces come off the blade, and even more as they come off the fence, the kerf widens considerably. I've had kerfs on compression wood spread to as much as 10 or 12 inches in a 6-foot-long board being ripped.

Reaction wood in deciduous trees forms on the upper side of the leaning trunk. The heartwood is less likely to be off-center, and the tension wood may well develop unevenly all around the trunk. Hardwood tension wood may show no signs other than a silvery or slightly dull color; however, the strength problem is the opposite of compression wood, with the wood having more than normal amounts of cellulose, thus being harder than normal. The fiber structure, though, doesn't cut as cleanly, so the surface is fuzzy looking. Stains blotch, and shrinkage along the length is, again, odd. The result is a funny looking fuzzed surface in a board that is almost certain to warp. If you note boards with a broom-like sweep to them, avoid buying the wood.

FUNGI

Fungi can screw up your materials before work starts and mess up your projects after the job's done. The best method of keeping low forms of plant life off woods is to eliminate the conditions under which they can grow. The parasites live principally off host plants, using the plant carbohydrates to feed themselves.

Molds work on wood surfaces, and one end of my house is currently awaiting an application of chlorine bleach, plus a mildewcide-heavy paint — to rid it of some of the worst mildew I've seen on a house. That's a combination of several damp, warm summers, damp moderately warm winters, and an improperly ventilated house (as far as walls, attic and similar spaces go). Your wood, before you buy it or after, is subject to mold on its surface, and *sap stains* internally. Molds wash off easily, with mildewcides to kill the parasite. Sap stains, with the characteristic bluish stain they leave behind, may die, but the effects remain. The discoloration is the main problem, not any structural difficulties.

Decay fungi actually dissolve cell walls, but except in very rare instances shouldn't be a problem in wood for woodworkers. With the fungi eating the wood cell walls in an enzymatic action, it takes a long time, and long exposure of wet wood, before the actual rot is formed. It is the condition some people totally misname dry rot. There is no such thing. Dry wood does not rot. Period.

Spalting is a sometimes desirable form of wood decay. Spalting occurs when some white rots attack some woods, resulting in thin lines of dark brown or black stain appearing in wildly variable patterns. This is also known as *zone-line decay*, because the lines outline pockets of decay and sound wood. You can make some unusually attractive items from spalted wood, if the wood has retained enough solidity to be machined.

We won't go further into dealing with fungi here, except to say that surface molds need to be eliminated as soon as they're discovered. This is most easily done with a mildewcide, which can be bought at any hardware store. Before that, either lower or raise the wood temperature for any fungus. Fungi grow best between 70° and 95°, with growth stopping at a low of 40° and a high of about 105°. Thus, kiln drying kills most fungi. Removal of oxygen also works, so keeping stored green wood moist — wood moisture content above 25 percent — works nicely, too. Any drying of wood should bring the moisture content *below* 20 percent as quickly as possible.

Fungi must also have food, and the carbohydrates in wood make it nearly ideal as a feeder station for one fungus or another. Where wood cannot be kept below 20 percent moisture content, then a resistant variety must be chosen, or treatment is needed. In most cases, we, as woodworkers, will not need treated wood or resistant wood, because our wood is quickly dried to as low as 6 percent moisture content, with the aim being stability in the assembled project, as well as elimination of fungi.

Chapter Two

NORTH AMERICAN SOFTWOODS

My emphasis in this chapter is on descriptions of the various easier-to-work, reasonable-in-cost softwoods that abound throughout the United States and Canada. Regardless of problems, which I look at only in passing in this book, this is one area of renewable resource care where replacements generally exceed takeouts. In other words, usually many more trees are planted than are cut. Of course, with the ever-increasing populations of almost all countries, such a policy is not just wise: It is essential to the future large-scale use of wood as a source of many present and future materials, plus continuation of its current widespread uses. There is a huge number of softwoods available to the woodworker, and the Forest Products Lab breaks the resulting lumber down into Western softwoods, and then, for the East, adds Northern and Southern softwoods. For our purposes, I'm going to clump them together, describing the weight, workability, appearance, tool requirements, price and availability of each species. In most cases I'm tossing in a small description of the trees as an extra measure, but you cannot identify the wood as logs at the sawmill, or when you buy logs,

from that description. It takes a great deal of knowledge and more time and space than we have in this book to render such identification accurately. Detailed ID of wood is not a purpose of this book, and even if it were, mistakes are possible when identifying wood primarily through visible grain features, ringing and bark. Even after all these years, I sometimes mistake elderly tulip (yellow) poplar for oak, for example. The older the poplar, the more likely I am to make the mistake. For truly accurate identification processes, you need Bruce Hoadley's *Identifying Wood*, which comes from Taunton Press and is available through most woodworker's mail order and retail outlets. It is the best material on the subject.

There are more than 750 species of North American trees, with 652 of them native species. There are many that are only a tiny bit different than another species nearby, but there are some extreme differences, too, as we'll see before we're through. While there is little point in covering some species—various small, bushlike trees that do not produce enough wood to interest most woodworkers—it doesn't pay to ignore too many species, because roots may make wonderful carving or turning stock. Manzanita (*Arctosta-*

phylos) is a notable example, and one I cannot find much reference material on. Well, to be honest, I can't find *any*. I've got a manzanita burl here, meant for turning, with a lovely, bright red-brown color. The wood is of medium hardness, and fairly easy to work, but that's all I can tell you. Because it is a species protected in California, I don't think you'll find a lot of information on it or the wood itself.

My classifications start with the cedars, and go on through cypress, fir, hemlock, larch, the pines, redwood, spruces, and arrives at tamarack. Some variations in the cedars are wide, while other woods—firs and pines for instance—are so similar in some ways they are often sold grouped as one type. (Southern pine is a group of four with very similar characteristics.)

Cedar, Alaska, is our alphabetical starting point for this group of durable softwoods. Growing in the Pacific Coast region of North America from southeastern Alaska down to southern Oregon (that's only three states, but geographically it's still a large range, because there's a long, long coastline involved), *Chamaecyparis nootkatensis* is straight-grained and finely textured, with sapwood white to a yellow shade, and a bright yellow sapwood. It is sometimes called yellow cedar, and is taken from a modest-sized tree—at least compared to others in the same forests—of about 80 to 100 feet in height. There is little difference in appearance of heartwood and sapwood. Alaska cedar is moderately heavy, very resistant to decay, and is moderately hard. After seasoning, during which it shrinks very little, the wood is quite stable. This is not one of our aromatic cedars, for its odor is mildly unpleasant when cut; it fades to a potato-like smell that isn't too bad. For interior finish work—moldings and such, furniture, small boats, cabinets and toys—Alaska cedar is an excellent choice. It works easily with both hand and power tools.

Cedar, Eastern Red, is another aromatic cedar, and grows about everywhere in the East except up into Maine and down into Florida. For some reason, it also stays away from much of the Gulf Coast, too, and out of the higher parts of the Appalachians. *Juniperus virginiana* is the major species of Eastern red cedar, but in some South Atlantic and Gulf Coastal Plains areas you will also find *Juniperus silicicola*. Either is sold as red cedar without further identification. The tree is small, usually not more than 40 feet tall, and it is slow growing. The heartwood of the red cedar is bright red, sometimes almost purple, tending to a duller red. The thin sapwood is almost white, and is clearly defined. The wood is moderately heavy, moderately low in strength and is hard. It seasons well, has high shock resistance and low stiffness, and a tight, fine texture. The grain is said to be straight, but after cutting hundreds of red cedars,

I've yet to see any run straight for much longer than a foot or two. The many, many knots deflect the grain. Red cedar, like all aromatic cedars, makes great chest linings (I recently built a walnut hope chest for an 18-year-old and lined it with *J. virginiana*, much to everyone's delight. The formal look of the raised walnut panels is relieved greatly by the red to white shading of the interior, and the resulting aroma, which may be renewed with an annual light sanding, is said to drive off moths). The wood is easily worked with conventional tools of all kinds, but will deposit lots of pitch if not seasoned well. Regardless, it lists as a nonresinous wood among botanical classifiers. It is quite stable when seasoned, and shrinks only a little while it is drying. Selected pieces make fine small boats and, as with the other aromatic cedars, it is great for small boxes and lining larger boxes.

Cedar, Incense is next on the parade of American cedars. *Libocedrus decurrens* is a California wood that works its way into southwestern Oregon and on to extreme western Nevada. Most of the lumber we see comes from northern California or southern Oregon. The tree may be 80 feet to as much as 150 feet in height, and 3 feet or more in diameter. The sapwood is white to a creamy color, and the heartwood is a light brown, frequently tingeing towards the red for a resulting pink overall tinge. The wood has a fine, uniform texture, and lives up to its name with a spicy aroma that wafts into the air when it is cut or sanded. Unlike Alaska cedar, and more like the remainder of American cedars, incense cedar is light in weight, fairly low in strength, with low shock resis-

tance (resistance to flex), and not a whole lot of stiffness (for a wood: Don't whack yourself on the head to test hardness or see if the board flexes). Shrinkage is modest, and there is little checking and warping during seasoning, so net lumber from green wood is a good figure. Incense cedar is locally low in cost, if you can accept its peckiness (localized pockets of decay that do not spread after the wood is dried) and other characteristics. It makes superb small box material, and lining material for larger boxes, cabinets and closets. The wood works easily with conventional (tool steel) and carbide tools.

Cedar, Port Orford, is sometimes called Lawson cypress; *Chamaecyparis lawsoniana* is also called Oregon cedar and white cedar. It grows in a narrow belt (never more than 40 miles inland) along the coast of Oregon, from Coos Bay south into California. Heartwood of Port Orford cedar is a light yellow shading to a pale brown, and sapwood is thin and hard to tell from the heartwood. The wood is nonresinous, slow growing, from a tree of large size, up to 160 feet in height and 5 feet in diameter. The wood is fine textured, with generally straight-grain, and a pleasant and spicy odor. If you haven't experienced the odor of any of these aromatic cedars, you have a distinct, and distinctive, treat coming. Port Orford cedar is superbly resistant to decay, moderately lightweight and is stiff, moderately strong and hard. Shock resistance is also in that middle range we call moderate. It is useful for lining blanket chests, making large and small boxes, making interior or exterior moldings and in boatbuilding. The wood works easily with a wide variety of conventional hand and power tools.

Cedar, Western Red. See "Gallery of Wood."

Cedar, white, Northern and Atlantic, are two distinct species that are usually clumped together at description time. Northern white cedar is *Thuja occidentalis* (also called, simply, cedar, and arbor vitae). Atlantic white cedar is *Chamaecyparis thyiodes* (also Southern white cedar, swamp cedar and boat cedar). Northern white cedar grows from Maine along the Appalachians, into the northern part of the Lake States. Atlantic white cedar grows along the Atlantic, or Right, Coast from Maine all the way down to northern Florida, and on west a ways. The latter is strictly a swamp tree. Production of Northern white cedar is heaviest in Maine and the Lake States, while swamp cedar is produced primarily in North Carolina and along the Gulf Coast. The trees are considerably smaller than Western red cedar trees, with the Northern white cedar reaching 50 to 65 feet, and not much over 18 to 24 inches in diameter. The Atlantic white cedar often reaches 65 feet, but may go to 90 or a bit more, with a straight trunk as much as 4 feet in diameter. White cedar heartwood is light brown, and the sapwood is nearly white, and forms only a thin band. The wood is lightweight, soft and not strong. Shock resistance is low, but shrinkage during seasoning is low and the wood is stable afterwards. This cedar takes paint well—most others require a coat of shellac to prevent bleed-through of resins—and like the rest of the cedars works easily with conventional tools, both hand and power. Heartwood is exceptionally durable, so the wood

is often used where great durability is essential, as in boats, tanks and woodenware that stays wet, or gets wet often.

The next step from cedars is to cypress, sometimes known as bald cypress.

Cypress is also called Southern cypress, red cypress, yellow cypress and white cypress. This is another deciduous—leaf-dropping—softwood, of medium size, rarely reaching 145 feet in height, and more often 65 to 130 feet. It has a buttressed trunk—cypress knees are famous as boat parts—that may be as much as 5 feet in diameter and reaching a rare dozen feet thick. The wood has become costly and is less available than in years gone by, and forced growth and current early growth heartwood cypress is not as durable as old-growth heartwood. Cypress is another tree with only a small sapwood band, which is nearly white, contrasting strongly with the light yellowish brown to dark reddish brown, brown, or even chocolate of the heartwood. *Taxodium distichum* is moderately heavy, moderately strong and moderately hard. This wood is moderate in just about every way except in its durability. It's also easy to work with conventional hand and power tools. It shrinks a bit more than cedars, but still within a very small range. Durability (decay resistance) ranges from truly great for old-growth cypress to moderate for new-growth materials. Fungus attacks the living trees, and creates a pecky condition that stabilizes on seasoning, so that pecky cypress is a very useful wood where you don't need water tightness, and appearance is not important—or, as in pan-

eling, if you want a different look. Cypress is great for general millwork, boxes of most sizes, shingles, molding and other uses. It makes a very unusual looking music box, for example. Unfortunately, you're apt to have a hard time locating cypress outside the Deep South, and even in some areas there, and you may end up having to pay a premium price for less than premium materials.

Firs come next in our taxonomy. There are Douglas firs, and true firs, in Eastern and Western divisions, to choose from, and they seem to mill around the country in profusion, and confusion. Most can be bought anywhere, often with species from 3,000 miles away taking precedence and holding a price advantage over more nearly local species. I'm glad I don't have to make sense of the pricing in the lumber industry.

Fir, Douglas, is sometimes called red fir, or yellow fir and, on infrequent occasions, Douglas spruce. The trees cover a wide range, from the Rocky Mountains to the Pacific Coast, and from Mexico to central British Columbia. Most production comes out of coastal states, Oregon, Washington and California, and from the Rocky Mountain States. Douglas fir is classed as an outstanding softwood throughout the world. Trees are commonly 150 to 180 feet tall, and may pass 200 feet. Diameters can exceed 6½ feet, but are more commonly 3 to 6 feet. *Pseudotsuga menziesii* has narrow sapwood in old-growth trees, though it may be as much as 3 inches wide in newer growth, even trees of commercial size. On older trees, the bark is often a foot thick. Fairly young trees have a reddish heartwood, and are the ones called red fir. Narrow-ringed wood on old trees is yellow-brown, and the wood is sometimes marketed as yellow fir. Weight and strength vary fairly widely but are stable enough that Douglas fir is used for building and construction and in plywood, as well as in sashes, doors, general millwork, boat construction and similar items, with its plywood used in all types of construction, furniture, cabinets and elsewhere. The wood works less than easily with common hand and power tools. Very sharp blades on power tools help reduce tear-out and splintering caused by the coarse texture. Douglas fir is fine for small projects or for structural elements of larger projects, especially structural elements that aren't going to be visible. Staining is a problem, though paint and clear finishes over unstained wood work well. Use a sealer before staining. The wood grips nails and screws well, and works nicely with all types of adhesives. It is very slightly resinous, so requires frequent cleaning of saw blades and other tools. Quartersawing Douglas fir helps to reduce splintering.

While the Douglas fir is a marvelous tree, it isn't a true fir. True firs are of the species *Abies*, and are found throughout much of North America. Most range from 60 to 120 feet tall, though the noble fir reaches 210 or more feet in height. None are resistant to fungi (pressure treatment is not as effective as with some other species). The wood is nonresinous and easy working with sharp tools. Pressure treatment of wood is a common procedure today, where wood is dried, then placed in pressure tanks and impregnated with chemicals — usually some form of chromated copper arsenate — under pressure.

The chemicals keep bugs, fungi and other nasties from eating the wood, thus making it far more durable. It is somewhat brittle, so sharp tools are needed to produce a good finish.

Firs, True (Eastern), consist of two species, balsam fir, or *Abies balsamea*, which is primarily a tree of New York, New England and Pennsylvania, plus the Lake States, and Fraser fir, or *A. fraseri*, which grows in the Virginia Appalachians, plus the Appalachians in North Carolina and Tennessee. Wood from true firs, both Western and Eastern species, is creamy white, shading to a pale brown, with heartwood and sapwood nearly impossible to tell apart. Balsam fir is lightweight, low in bending and compressive strength, soft, and low in shock resistance. Eastern firs mainly make pulpwood, though in New England and the Lake States some lumber is produced from them.

Firs, True (Western), include six species: subalpine fir, or *Abies lasiocarpa*; California red fir, or *A. grandis*; noble fir, or *A. procera*; Pacific silver fir, or *A. amabilis*; and white fir, or *A. concolor*. Western firs are also light in weight, but, except for subalpine fir, are stronger than balsam fir. Shrinkage is small to moderate. Western true firs are cut for lumber in Washington, Oregon, California, western Montana and northern Idaho, and marketed as white fir throughout the United States. High-grade noble fir is used for interior finish and moldings, and most firs go into general construction lumber, boxes, crates, sash, doors and general millwork. Ladder rails are often made from noble fir. Like Eastern true firs, the wood is readily worked

with normal, standard hand and power tools.

The U.S. and Canada share two species of hemlocks. North America is the only source of commercial hemlock timber, though tree hemlock grows in Asia. Western hemlock is commercially the most important of the two species, and the wood is more attractive. The Western hemlock is a large tree, up to 180 feet in height; the Eastern hemlock is considerably smaller.

Hemlock, Eastern, grows from New England to northern Alabama and Georgia and into the Lake States, as well as into eastern Quebec and southern Maritime Provinces. *Tsuga canadensis* is also known as Canadian hemlock and hemlock spruce, and is a moderate tree in size, topping out around 80 feet tall and 3 feet in diameter. Production is split about evenly between New England, the Middle Atlantic and the Lake States. Heartwood of Eastern hemlock is pale brown, with a reddish tint. The sapwood doesn't form an easily identifiable separation from the heartwood, but may shade to a lighter color. Hemlock is coarse textured and uneven, moderately lightweight, moderately hard, moderately low in strength, moderately low in shock resistance and moderately limber. The wood is used for lumber and pulpwood, with the lumber used primarily for building framing, sheathing, subflooring, and in the making of pallets and boxes. Though not of great interest to the woodworker, Eastern hemlock may serve for small projects and as parts of larger projects. It works well with regular tools, but is subject to tear-out in crosscutting; resin buildup is quite low. Screws and nails and glues all hold well. Eastern hemlock doesn't take finishes as well as the western variety, because of its coarser texture.

Hemlock, Western, is also known as West Coast hemlock, Pacific hemlock, British Columbia hemlock, hemlock spruce and Western hemlock-fir. Like Eastern hemlock and many of the firs, Western hemlock is often sold as one of a grouping called hem-fir when it has reached the stage of being lumber. It grows along the Pacific Coast of Oregon and Washington, and in the northern Rockies, north to Canada and Alaska. *Tsuga heterophylla* has a relative, mountain hemlock *(T. mertensiana)* that inhabits mountainous country from central California to Alaska. Heartwood and sapwood are almost white, with a slight purplish tint, and the sapwood is somewhat lighter colored, and generally not more than an inch thick. The wood frequently has small, sound black knots that are usually tight and stay in place. Dark streaks found in the lumber are caused by hemlock bark maggots, and do not normally reduce wood strength. Western hemlock is moderately light in weight, and moderate in strength. Hardness, stiffness and shock resistance are all moderate, too. Shrinkage is moderately large, about the same as Douglas fir, but green hemlock contains more water than Douglas fir, and thus requires more kiln drying time to reach the same percentage of dryness. Mountain hemlock is similar in properties, but is a bit lower in bending strength and stiffness. Western hemlock's principal uses are as lumber and in plywood, and end uses are sheathing, siding, subflooring, joists, studs,

planks, rafters, boxes, pallets, crates and small amounts for furniture and ladders. For the average woodworker, it's not a greatly attractive wood, but does a nice job for larger projects that need frames. It works well with conventional hand and power tools and glues readily. It also takes finishes well after accepting sanding to a silky smooth surface.

Before we reach the widest array of softwoods in this country, the pines, we have one short stop at larch.

Larches are unusual among softwoods, as they drop their leaves in winter. The tree may reach 120 feet, with a trunk a yard in diameter, so it is a medium-sized tree (for a softwood).

Larch, Western, grows in western Montana, northern Idaho, northeastern Oregon, and on the eastern slope of Washington's Cascade Mountains. The largest percentage of *Larix occidentalis*, about 65 percent, is produced in Idaho and Montana, with the rest coming from Oregon and Washington. Heartwood of Western larch is yellowish brown, and the sapwood a yellow-white. The sapwood is generally 1 inch or less thick, and the wood is stiff, moderately strong and hard, moderately high in shock resistance and moderately heavy. Shrinkage is moderately large in this straight-grained wood, and distortion during drying can be a problem. The wood splits easily and is subject to ring shake. Ring shake is a cup-shaped—cup is an inward curl of the wood—splitting of the wood along the growth rings. Most shakes are radial, or across the growth rings, and any shake is a split in the wood. Knots are common, but

are usually small and tight. Western larch is useful primarily for rough-dimension building lumber, small timbers, planks and boards, and the lumber is sometimes sold mixed with Douglas fir, which has similar properties. Some of the best material is made into interior finish products, sashes and doors. For woodworking purposes, it is most commonly used in framing of projects. Conventional tools are all you need here, either hand or power, for this reasonably durable wood.

Pines are the woods most of us are familiar with, both as woodworkers and as people living in homes with wood products. Pines are more prolific now than any other wood, and are probably used for more things than most other woods. They come in species that are very soft and low in strength, that are still strong enough for building construction, and that accept shaping amazingly well, so that a great many items from toys to doors are produced from pine today, as they have been for centuries—and will be for centuries to come. And they come in species that are almost as hard as a midrange hardwood (many of the yellow pines), that do not take nails easily, and that are not as easy to shape, but that are wonderfully strong and useful in many ways. Here, I'll look at several of the numerous varieties of pine to be found in the United States and Canada. Other pines may be locally used, but these are the largest commercial varieties for several reasons: First, they're widespread, though many are now planted in commercial stands; second, they have the useful features most needed by the largest number of builders and woodworkers; and third, they're fairly fast growing as trees go.

Pine, Eastern White. See "Gallery of Wood."

Pine, Jack, is also called scrub pine, gray pine or black pine in the United States, and it grows naturally in the Lake States and in a few areas of New England and New York. *Pinus banksiana* is often marketed with the other pines among which it grows. Sapwood is nearly white, with a light brown heartwood that tends towards the orange. Sapwood makes up as much as half the volume of the tree, and the wood is coarse in texture and quite resinous. It is moderately light in weight, moderately low in bending strength and compressive strength, and has a moderately low resistance to shock. It is low in stiffness, as well, but shrinks only modestly. The lumber is generally knotty, and jack pine is most useful for pulpwood, box lumber, pallets and similar applications. It works easily with conventional tools, but creates possible problems with resin buildup even with seasoned wood.

Pine, Lodgepole, is also called knotty pine, black pine, spruce pine and jack pine. *Pinus contorta* grows in the Rockies, and in the Pacific Coast regions as far north as Alaska. Production of lodgepole pine comes from the Rocky Mountain States, Idaho, Montana, Oregon and Washington. Heartwood of lodgepole pine swings from a light yellow to a light yellow-brown, and the sapwood is yellow to white. Wood is usually straight-grained. Lodgepole pine is moderately lightweight, fairly easy to work, and has moderately large shrinkage. It rates as moderately low in strength, moderately

soft, moderately stiff, and moderately low in shock resistance. It is, like most pines, easy to work if conventional hand and power tools are kept clear of large amounts of pitch buildup. Wood is mostly used for framing, poles, crossties, siding, some finish stock and flooring. It is not strongly useful to the woodworker, and is mentioned mostly because it sometimes becomes available locally at a very low price. At such times, top quality black pine is great for toy and small furniture projects.

Pine, Longleaf, or *Pinus palustris*, grows from eastern North Carolina south to Florida, and west into eastern Texas. Shortleaf pine, or *P. echinata*, grows from southeastern New York and New Jersey south into northern Florida and west into eastern Texas and Oklahoma. Loblolly pine, or *P. taeda*, grows from Maryland south through the Atlantic Coastal Plain and Piedmont Plateau into Florida and west into eastern Texas. Slash pine, or *P. elliottii*, grows in Florida and the southern parts of South Carolina, Georgia, Alabama, Mississippi and Louisiana east of the Mississippi River. Industry grading standards class the lumber of those species, and some other very minor species, as Southern pine. The lumber comes primarily from the Southern and South Atlantic States, with Georgia, Alabama, North Carolina, Arkansas and Louisiana leading production. The wood of the species is similar in appearance, with reddish brown heartwood and a yellow-white sapwood. Sapwood is wider in second-growth stands, but in older, slow-growth trees, sapwood may be only an inch or two thick. Southern pines are heavy, strong, stiff, hard, and moder-

ately high in shock resistance. The shortleaf types are slightly lighter in weight. All have moderately large shrinkage, but are stable when properly dried. The Southern Forest Products Association has strict grading standards, including wood density ratings. Uses are extremely wide, from building material such as sheathing and subflooring on through cooperage (that's barrels to us noncoopers), railroad crossties, piles, posts, trusses and joists. Much of it is pressure-treated, and probably 95 percent of the decks and porches throughout the South are made of treated Southern pine. The wood is harder to work than other pines and resists nail penetration about like locust, but otherwise it is easy to work with conventional hand and power tools. Pitch buildup is moderate.

Pine, Pitch, is the pine most closely associated with "hollers" and "hardscrabble," I think. *Pinus rigida* is found along the mountain spine from Maine through northern Georgia, and is a resinous wood with a brownish red heartwood. The sapwood is thick and a light yellow, while the wood of the pitch pine is moderately heavy fringing towards heavy, moderately strong, stiff and hard, with moderately high shock resistance. Shrinkage is moderately small to moderately large, and use is mostly lumber and pulpwood. The wood works easily with conventional hand and power tools, but the buildup of resin is quick and must be cleared from blades frequently.

Pine, Pond, grows from Florida north to New Jersey, keeping to coastal regions. The wood is heavy and coarse-grained, with dark orange-colored heartwood, and yellow, thick sapwood. Shrinkage in this very resinous wood is moderately large, and it is moderately strong, stiff and moderately hard, with moderately high shock resistance. Used mostly for general construction, *Pinus serotina* also makes good poles, posts and railway crossties. It works well with conventional tools, but pitch buildup is fast and heavy.

Pine, Ponderosa, is known as Western soft pine, Western yellow pine, bull pine and blackjack pine. *Pinus ponderosa* has a companion tree, the Jeffrey pine *(P. jeffreyi)*, that grows in close association and is marketed under the same name. The ponderosa pine is another large tree, often reaching 230 feet in height, with a trunk about 30 inches in diameter. Major growth areas are California, Oregon and Washington, with smaller amounts coming from the southern Rockies, the Black Hills of South Dakota and Wyoming. This is a true yellow pine, not a white pine, but a large proportion of the wood is similar to white pine in appearance and properties. The heartwood is a light reddish brown, and the wide sapwood band is nearly white, varying to pale yellow. Wood of the outer portions of the tree is moderately lightweight, moderately low in strength, moderately soft, moderately stiff, and moderately low in shock resistance. It is usually straight-grained, and has modest shrinkage during drying. The wood is uniform in texture with little tendency to warp or twist. It is used mainly for lumber, and to a small extent for veneers, poles, posts and so forth, but clear wood makes sash, mantels, moldings, paneling and cabinets. Low-grade material goes into boxes and crates. Much of the wood now goes into particleboard and papermaking. It works very nicely with conventional hand and power tools and resin buildup is within reason. (It always pays to keep clearing resin when working with pines, cedars, and other sometimes nonresinous woods that have sticky sap.) This wood can be painted or varnished, but is best finished after using a sealer. It does finish out exceptionally well for a softwood.

Pine, Red, is often called Norway pine, and on occasion is also called hard pine and pitch pine. *Pinus resinosa* grows in New England, New York, Pennsylvania and the Lake States. Heartwood is pale red varying to reddish brown, while the nearly white sapwood may have a yellowish tinge. Sapwood is from 2 to 4 inches wide. The wood resembles lighter weight Southern pine. Latewood is distinct in the growth rings. Red pine is moderately heavy, moderately strong and stiff, moderately soft, and moderately high in shock resistance. Generally, it is straight-grained, but not as uniform in texture as Eastern white pine. It is resinous, but not extremely so. Shrinkage is moderately large, but kiln drying isn't difficult and the wood is stable when seasoned. Used principally for lumber, red pine also makes pilings, poles, cabin logs and other items. It goes into sash, doors, general millwork and crates. The wood is easy to work with conventional hand and power tools. Resin buildup is moderate.

Pine, Southern, is actually a group of species that have similar characteristics and grow in many of the same areas. There are four major species in the Southern pine grouping, which is sometimes classed overall as pitch pine (mostly by Europeans who seem to think all American woods should equate to European woods in variety, weight, tree size and name). Trees range up to 90 and even 100 feet in height, and trunks are as much as 36 inches in diameter. Southern pines are moderately durable and also take treatment well, so that pressure-treated Southern pine is a truly long-lasting wood for almost all uses. All tend to build up resin on tools.

Pine, Spruce, is also known as cedar pine, poor pine, Walter pine and bottom white pine. *Pinus glabra* is classed as one of the minor Southern pine species, and grows most commonly on low, wet lands of the coastal areas of southeastern South Carolina, Georgia, Alabama, Mississippi, Louisiana, and into northern and northwestern Florida. Heartwood is a light brown, and the wide sapwood is very close to white. Spruce pine is lower than most of the major Southern pine species for strength values, but compares favorably with white fir in many areas. Plywood is a major use these days. It works easily with conventional tools, and has a moderate pitch buildup.

Pine, Sugar, is the world's largest species of pine, and is sometimes called California sugar pine. Trees sometimes reach 150 feet in height, with trunks over 3 feet in diameter. Most lumber is produced in California, with some from southwestern Oregon. *Pinus lambertiana* has a buff to light brown heartwood, sometimes tending towards the red. Sapwood is a creamy white, and the wood is straight-grained, fairly even in texture, and very easy to work with conventional hand or power tools, if the tools are kept sharp. Dull tools tear the wood. Shrinkage is small, and the wood seasons well without checking or warping. It is also stable when seasoned, and is lightweight, moderately low in strength, moderately soft, low in shock resistance and low in stiffness. Sugar pine is used primarily for lumber products, with most going to boxes, crates, sash, doors, frames, general millwork, building construction and foundry patterns. Like Eastern white pine, sugar pine is suitable for use in nearly every part of a house because of its working ease, its ability to remain in place, and its easy nailing properties. It is also superb for the woodworker, as a moderately priced, clear, usable wood for many projects, from furniture to toys. It glues well and finishes nicely, too.

Pine, Virginia, *P. virginiana,* is also called Jersey pine and scrub pine, and grows from New Jersey and Virginia on through the Appalachian region to Georgia and the Ohio Valley. This is another minor species of the Southern pine classification, with orange heartwood, and almost white sapwood that is relatively thick. The wood is moderately heavy, moderately strong, moderately hard, and moderately stiff, with moderately high shrinkage in drying. It is used for railroad ties, mine timbers, pulpwood and lumber. It works fairly easily with conventional tools, both hand and power, but is best worked with carbide-edged tools. Pitch buildup is heavy.

Pine, Western White, is known as Idaho white pine, or, simply, white pine. This medium-sized tree may reach 125 feet, with a 3-foot-diameter trunk. About 80 percent of the cut comes from Idaho with a little bit from Montana and Oregon, and the rest from Washington. The heartwood of *Pinus monticola* is a cream color to light reddish brown that darkens on exposure to light and air. (A number of woods do this: Cherry in the hardwoods is a specific example, and the darkening extends over a year or so, which is why I don't like to stain cherry.) The sapwood of Western white pine is 1 to 3 inches wide, and yellow-white. The wood is straight-grained, easy to work, easily kiln dried and stable after drying. It is moderately low in strength, moderately soft, moderately stiff, moderately low in shock resistance and lightweight. It glues easily and finishes well. Shrinkage is moderately large, but the wood, as noted, is stable after drying. Most all of it becomes lumber, with normal wide uses in building construction, matches, boxes, patterns and millwork products. Some is made into siding, and exterior and interior trim and finish. Overall a marvelous wood for boxes, furniture, toys and many other woodworking projects, Western white pine also is relatively low cost and requires only conventional tools.

Next we have one of the most famous, and most controversial, woods around today. It appears to have become, at least in some ways, the equivalent of rain forest woods to a lot of people in the United States. I support many conservation efforts that have reasonable aims, though some of the reported activities of the environmental activist groups involved with preservation of the redwood forests involve activities that are clearly beyond reason.

The redwood is the fastest-growing conifer there is, and one of the longest-lived trees. Cost can be a little rocky for those of us in the East, but for outdoor projects, there's little natural wood to beat it.

There's also a lot to say for redwood in woodworking outside of its usual arena of deck and fence construction. I recently built a couple of redwood bookcases, and the warm beauty of the wood is incredible. It doesn't put cherry or walnut to shame, but certainly gives a different look to the room. Redwood can be a good carving wood, too, but its straight grain makes it susceptible to splitting. Very sharp tools and a little extra care reduce possible problems: Make sure you crosscut with a very fine-toothed, sharp blade to prevent tear-out. Ripping requires little or no special technique or blade. I generally use a 24-tooth (10-inch) blade with a good edge and allow no resin buildup so that I get a fine glue-line cut. Much depends on immediate conditions, but cleaning resin from the blade after every couple dozen feet of cutting can help.

Redwood is a very large tree, growing along the coast of California. Tree size is often in the 300-foot range, with trunks nearly 10 feet in diameter. That is a large tree by all standards! (Europeans do not want it confused with *their* redwood, which is a species of pine that is considerably heavier, far different in appearance, from a small tree, and at least 6,000 miles away.) *Sequoia sempervirens* has a closely related species, giant sequoia *(Sequoiadendron giganteum),* that grows in a very limited area of the Sierra Nevada of California. Use of the giant sequoia is very limited. Redwood is also called Coast redwood, California redwood and sequoia. The heartwood of redwood varies from a light cherry red to a dark mahogany color, and the narrow sapwood is almost white. Old-growth redwood is moderately light in weight, moderately strong and stiff and moderately hard. The wood is easy to work, is generally very straight-grained, and shrinks and swells very little. Heartwood from old-growth trees has extremely high decay resistance, but heartwood from second-growth trees ranges from resistant to moderately resistant. Most redwood lumber is used for building, and it is made into siding, sash, doors, finish and containers. It is used for all sorts of tanks, silos, cooling towers and outdoor furniture where durability is important. Redwood is absolutely great for many smaller outdoor woodworking projects, including birdhouses and feeders. The wood splits easily, and some products are made from those splits—post and rail fences, for example. At one time, plywood was manufactured, but my sources tell me, without specifying a reason, that no more is being made. The wood works easily with conventional power or hand tools, and resin buildup is slight. The wood splits, but doesn't splinter easily, so you can often work with less damage to your hands. When you do get a splinter, though, the resin needs to be cleared quickly from the wound—I use a peroxide boil: Simply keep pouring peroxide on until it quits foaming, wait thirty minutes and do it again.

Next are the spruces. There are five with which we need some familiarity in woodworking.

Spruces provide light-colored, reasonably strong wood that can go into building construction or pulpwood, or into cabinets; the Engelmann spruce, with no characteristic odor of its own, makes excellent food containers.

Spruce, Eastern, is a group of three species that are very much alike. Red *(Picea rubens)*, white *(P. glauca)* and black *(P. mariana)* spruces are sold as a single species, usually for pulpwood. The wood dries easily and is stable after drying, with moderately light weight, easy working characteristics, moderate shrinkage and moderate strength. It is light in color, with little difference visible between the heartwood and sapwood. The largest use for Eastern spruce is pulpwood, but some does find its way into building construction, general millwork, boxes, crates, and even piano sounding boards.

Spruce, Engelmann, grows at high elevations in the Rockies. Other names for *Picea engelmanni* include white spruce, mountain spruce, Arizona spruce, silver spruce and balsam. About 65 percent of the lumber comes from the southern Rocky Mountain States, with the rest coming from the northern Rocky Mountain States and Oregon. The heartwood of the Engelmann spruce is nearly white, with a very slight tint of red. Sapwood ranges up to 2 inches in width and is hard to tell from the heartwood. The wood has a medium to fine texture, and no characteristic taste or odor of its own. It is usually straight-grained, and is rated as lightweight. It is low in strength, whether as a beam or a post, and is limber, soft, and low in shock resistance. Shrinkage is small to moderate. Typically, the lumber contains many small knots. Engelmann spruce is used primarily for lumber, mine timbers, railroad crossties and poles. In building construction, it takes the form of sheathing and studs. It also has great properties for pulp and papermaking. While not as good for woodworking uses as other light woods, Engelmann spruce is fine for toys, and small furniture projects where knots may be avoided or incorporated into the project pattern.

Spruce, Sitka, is a large tree that grows along the northwestern coast of North America, from California to Alaska. It often reaches 290 feet tall, and has a buttressed trunk up to 16 feet in diameter. Forest-grown trees are generally smaller in size, but still large. *Picea sitchensis* is also known as yellow spruce, tideland spruce, Western spruce, silver spruce and West Coast spruce. The Alaska production mostly goes to the Orient, while material for our use is produced in Washington and Oregon. Sitka spruce heartwood is a light, pinkish brown, and the sapwood is creamy white and shades gradually into the heartwood. The sapwood may be 6 inches wide. The wood has a fine, uniform texture, and is generally straight-grained, with no distinct taste or odor. It is moderately light in weight, moderately low in bending and compressive strength, moderately stiff, and moderately low in shock resistance. Shrinkage is moderately small, and straight, clear-grained pieces are easily obtained. Principal uses are lumber, furniture, millwork and boats. It is important in small aircraft production, and also is used as ladder rails and for piano sounding boards. It works very nicely indeed with sharp conventional hand and power tools; dull tools tear the earlywood. It makes superb boxes of almost any size, and the lack of taste and odor makes it excellent for canisters and similar projects. It is great for paneled projects, too, and glues up nicely. It takes stain fairly well, and takes good finishes with both paint and varnish. However, Sitka spruce is definitely on the costly side for softwoods.

Tamarack grows from Maine across to Minnesota, with most of the stand in the Lake States. Heartwood is yellowish brown shading to a russet brown, with a whitish sapwood less than an inch thick. Wood is coarsely textured and has no odor or taste. Transition from earlywood to latewood is abrupt, and *Larix laricina* wood falls in the midrange for most of its properties. Currently, most use seems to be as pulpwood, then lumber, tank construction and boxes. For the woodworker, it is another wood suitable for food containers, such as canisters, because it has no properties of its own to add to the contents. Tree size and wood characteristics are very much like those of larch, described earlier.

GALLERY OF
POPULAR
WOOD

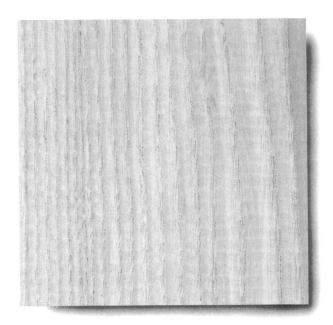

ASH
(hardwood)

BASSWOOD
(hardwood)

There are many species of ash, including white ash *(Fraxinus americana)*, green ash *(F. pennsylvanica)*, blue ash *(F. quadrangulata)*, black ash *(F. nigra)*, pumpkin ash *(F. profunda)* and Oregon ash *(F. latifolia)*. The Oregon ash is the only one of the six native to the West. Commercial species are mostly made up of white and green ash, though blue ash is sometimes added. Ash trees tend to be medium to large in size, ranging up to 110 feet. The wood is straight-grained, sometimes with a wavy grain that aids its appearance. It dries readily with moderate shrinkage, and is relatively stable after seasoning. It is not durable, but bends when steamed as well or better than most wood. Nail- and screw-holding power is high, and gluing presents no difficulties. The wood takes a nice finish and sands easily. Darken it slightly, and ash resembles oak. Black ash has the most interesting grain and figuring, generally. (Black ash may be marketed as brown ash.) Heartwood is brown, and the sapwood is very light, almost white. Second-growth white ash is heavy, strong, hard, stiff, and has a high resistance to shock. Because of these qualities, ash is used for handles, oars, baseball bats, and projects where shock is a constant. Ash is superb for projects that will contain or contact food, such as canisters and cutting boards. Black ash is important in the Lake States, and is much lighter than white ash. Lighter weight ash wood is often sold as cabinet ash, and is great for furniture and most woodworking projects.

Basswood grows in the eastern half of the United States and Canada, southward. Most basswood lumber comes from the Lake, Middle Atlantic and Central States. The tree is medium-sized, to about 65 feet tall, with a diameter of about 2 feet. Heartwood is pale yellow-brown with some darker streaks. Basswood has wide, creamy-colored or pale brown sapwood that merges gradually into the heartwood. When seasoned, the wood has neither odor nor taste. It is soft, light in weight, and of a fine, even texture. The wood is straight-grained and easy to work with hand tools. It holds detail well in carving, so the wood is the premier choice of most carvers. Shrinkage in width and thickness during drying is large, but basswood seldom warps after seasoning. The wood takes finishes well, except for stains, which blotch, and holds nails and screws well. It is easy to glue. Basswood is often used in apiary supplies (bee hives, etc.), door frames, molding, woodenware, cooperage, and for veneer and pulpwood. It is a good wood for children to start on, for it is virtually effort-free to work. Cost is moderate, running about 25 percent less than the oaks. American Basswood is the most important of the native basswood species. *Tila americana* is followed in importance by white basswood, *T. heterophylla*. They are sold with no attempt to differentiate between the two.

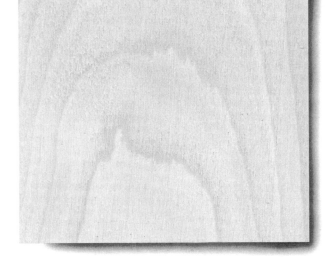

BEECH
(hardwood)

BIRCH
(hardwood)

American Beech grows in the eastern third of the United States and up into abutting Canadian provinces. The greatest production of beech lumber is in the Central and Middle Atlantic States. The tree is moderately large at 120 feet, with a trunk about 48 inches in diameter, in prime growing conditions. The bark is smooth, almost like a tight skin, silver-gray and disfigured here and there with darker gray spots. Wood color varies from white sapwood to a reddish brown heartwood, with little or no demarcation visible between the types. Sapwood may be 5 inches thick. Beech wood has little figure and is of close, uniform texture, with no characteristic taste or odor. Grain is straight, and the wood is not durable in weather. Beech is classed as a heavy, hard and strong, high shock resistant wood that is great for steam bending. *Fagus grandifolia* shrinks substantially during seasoning, so needs careful drying to prevent excessive loss from distortion. It also tends to move a lot under changing humidity conditions. Beech works well with hand and power tools. Nails and screws hold well. Beech glues easily and stains and polishes well. Most beech goes into flooring, brush blocks, handles, veneer, woodenware, cooperage, containers and similar products, but because it is difficult to dry, a great deal also goes into pulpwood and clothespins. Beech heartwood and sapwood have markedly different expansion and contraction rates, so cannot be mixed in a project unless you enjoy repairing joints and splits.

Woodworker's most poular birches are yellow birch *(Betula alleghaniensis)*, paper birch *(B. papyrifera)* and sweet birch *(B. lenta)*. River birch *(B. nigra)*, gray birch *(B. populifolia)* and Western paper birch *(B. papyrifera var. commutata)* make up the remaining mix. The first three grow mainly in the Northeastern and Lake States and into the adjoining Canadian provinces. Yellow and sweet birch also grow along the Appalachians down to northern Georgia. These are the source of most birch lumber and veneer. Yellow birch is the largest of the trees, often reaching 65 feet, with trunks to 30 inches in diameter. Yellow birch has white sapwood and light, red-brown heartwood, while sweet birch's light-colored sapwood meets a dark brown heartwood tinged in red. Paper birch is a slightly smaller tree, about 60 feet in height and up to 2 feet in diameter. The wood from sweet and yellow birch trees is hard, heavy and strong. It has good shock resistance and a fine, uniform texture, but is not durable. Paper birch is lighter, softer and not as strong. Birch holds nails and screws well, glues well, and is fairly easy to machine with power tools. It can be difficult to work with hand tools, and machine working is far easier. Birch stains nicely if a sealer is used, but tends to blotch without one. After sealing it can be polished out to a fine finish. Birch shrinks a lot when curing. Yellow and sweet birch lumber and veneer go mainly into furniture, boxes, woodenware, interior finish products, paneling, electronics cabinets and doors.

BUBINGA
(exotic wood)

BUTTERNUT
(hardwood)

ften called African rosewood (it is not a rosewood, which requires membership in the *Dalbergia genus*), bubinga comes from West Africa. The trees are of medium size, up to about 100 feet, with long trunks sometimes almost 40 inches in diameter. Heartwood from *Guibourtia tessmanni, G. demeusei, G. pellegriniana* is pink, vivid red, or red-brown with purple streaks. The latter becomes yellow or medium brown with a red tint when exposed to light and air. Sapwood is a creamy vanilla in appearance. Great density and fine texture are features of bubinga. Moderately hard and very heavy, bubinga works well with machine or hand tools. Drying can be difficult, but taking time means the wood seasons out nicely, with moderate losses. The wood is useful in turnery, flooring, furniture, cabinetwork and decorative veneers. A few years ago, I got hold of a piece of bubinga and used it as part of a model piano-music box. It truly is easy to work, requiring only sharp tools, and glues nicely. It takes clear finishes with no problems, and anyone who stains it probably should be run out of town. Availability is currently good, but some countries are limiting cutting, which will eventually drive up the currently moderate price (bubinga costs about one to three dollars a board foot more than walnut at the moment). Toxicity appears to be low.

Also known as white walnut butternut, closely resembles black walnut when stained. *Juglans cinerea* grows from southern New Brunswick, into Maine and west to Minnesota, with a southern range down into northeastern Arkansas and east to western North Carolina. Butternut is a medium-sized tree, reaching almost 100 feet under prime conditions, with a diameter to 4 feet. European sources state a height of 50 feet, but one has to wonder where they got the information: The largest currently listed butternut is 90-plus feet tall. Butternut is a short-lived tree, lasting from 60 to 80 years. Sapwood is narrow and almost white, with heartwood a light brown showing some pink tones or dark brown streaks. Butternut wood is lightweight—not much heavier than Eastern white pine—and coarse textured, and moderately weak in bending and vertical or endwise compression. It is also relatively low in stiffness and fairly soft, with moderately high shock resistance. Butternut machines easily with both power and hand tools, finishes well and takes glue well. Sharp tools help prevent tearout of the soft fibers. It holds nails and screws securely, and closely resembles black walnut when stained to match. It does not, of course, come close to matching walnut's strength or hardness. Butternut is a furniture, cabinet, paneling, trim and veneer wood, but may be hard to find commercially because most woodworkers don't ask for it—though carvers do.

CEDAR, WESTERN RED
(softwood)

CHERRY
(hardwood)

This wood can be found in the Pacific Northwest and along the Pacific, or Left, Coast to Alaska. *Thuja plicata* is also called canoe cedar, giant arbor vitae, shinglewood and Pacific red cedar. Principal production is in Washington, but much comes from Oregon, Idaho and Montana. The tree may reach heights of 160 feet and more, and be 4 feet and more in diameter. The aroma is pungently attractive. Heartwood of the Western red cedar lumber is a reddish brown to a dull brown, and the sapwood is nearly white, and narrow, seldom forming a band more than an inch thick. The wood is generally straight, but has a coarse and uniform texture. Shrinkage is slight, and the resulting wood is light in weight, moderately soft, low in strength, and the heartwood is exceptionally resistant to decay. Shock resistance is low. Primary uses are for shingles, boxes, boatbuilding, greenhouse construction, millwork and similar items. You may wish to use it to make small boxes, cabinets, small boats, or most other items where low beam strength is not an important criterion. Western red cedar works easily — most red cedar shakes are hand-split — with all conventional tools, both hand and power.

Prunus serotina is scattered from southeastern Canada throughout the eastern half of the United States. Production is chiefly centered in the Middle Atlantic States.

Cherry is a moderate-sized tree, reaching about 90 to 100 feet, with a possible 54-inch trunk diameter. Cherry heartwood is a medium red-brown with its own characteristic luster. Sapwood is narrow and nearly white. Grain is straight, finely textured and close, with, usually, a gentle waving figure. Ripple and quilt patterns sometimes crop up, too. Cherry has a uniform texture and excellent machining properties, except for a strong tendency to burn if dull tools or a too-slow feed (with power tools) are used. Oddly enough, high-speed steel (HSS) blades seem to create less of a burning problem than do carbide-tipped blades. Use slow drill press speeds (250 rpm or even 200) and do not pause or, again, you'll get some burning. Do not use twist drills; they always create burn marks. You may also find some sap pockets in cherry and should avoid them when possible. It is a medium-heavy, strong, stiff, moderately hard wood, with high shock resistance. Cherry shrinks a lot when drying, but is very stable after it is seasoned. Cherry glues well, but is affected strongly by excess glue squeeze-out — it mars the finished work badly when clear finishes are applied. Do not cross-grain sand. It creates scratches. Cherry finishes beautifully, but requires some thought. You probably aren't going to want to stain a wood that has a natural tendency to darken over time.

COCOBOLO
(exotic wood)

EBONY
(exotic wood)

From the same genus as rosewood, *Dalbergia Retusa*, cocobolo is the Central Amerian variant. While the other parts of the genus prefer the rain forests of South America, cocobolo thrives in the drier upland country of Central America's Pacific coast. Cocobolo doesn't form a majestic tree, reaching no more than 80 feet, with a 3-foot-diameter trunk and an overall poor shape. Cocobolo is a wood too dense to float. Heartwood may carry a wide range of shades, including red, yellow, pink and black, with the occasional, but not really infrequent, streaks of green, purple and blue. The sapwood is a creamy white. Cocobolo is best worked with power tools or exceptionally sharp hand tools; for power tools, use carbide, or you'll spend a lot of time sharpening edges. Sanding and polishing bring out an exceptional luster in the wood. Nail- and screw-gripping power is great, and splitting isn't a problem, but you must drill pilot holes to reduce work. Gluing is difficult, because the wood, like rosewood, contains a lot of oils, plus silica. Wipe all mating surfaces with lacquer thinner or alcohol—even acetone might help. Cocobolo makes great handles, mirror backs, turned items and similar projects, but should never be used for food-handling projects, or in any project that requires touching the wood to the lips—recorders and similar musical instruments are best made of some other wood.

Although incredibly expensive, ebony is rare and unique in color. It is the only truly black wood I know of. The tree is small, seldom over 15 feet in height, with a trunk diameter of as much as 30 inches. Sapwood is yellowish white, and heartwood of *Diospyros spp.* is jet-black in its most desirable form, but may also be a medium-brown to dark brown with black stripes. It is fine and even in texture, and extremely heavy. Ebony does not work or handle easily. It takes great care in drying, and is hard and brittle after drying. The heartwood is durable, something that probably won't matter since I've never seen it used in any sort of outdoor project. It is too costly and too specialized for outdoor uses. Ebony does not glue well. It can, with care and sharp tools, be brought to a truly excellent finish. Ebony is also a superb turning wood. The wood is used in turnery, musical instruments, cutlery handles and inlays.

GONCALO ALVES
(exotic wood)

Both *Astronium graveolons* and *A. fraxinifolium* are found through the area from Brazil, but the species range from southern Mexico through Central America and into the Amazon Basin. The wood is also known as tigerwood, zebrawood and kingwood. The tree is of medium size, close to 100 feet, and produces a trunk about 3 feet in diameter. Fresh heartwood is russet, orange brown, or red-brown to red, with narrow to wide irregular stripes of medium to very dark brown. The wood is hard, medium-textured and very dense even when air dried. It is very strong, with strength values higher than most well-known United States woods. In most cases, disregarding the strength of the wood, it is imported for its beauty. The heartwood is very durable. Grain varies from straight to wavy and interlocked. Goncalo alves is difficult to work, but has a natural luster and polishes to a superb finish. Carbide tool edges are almost essential, but the wood turns nicely if tools are kept sharp, and it glues up well. It holds screws and nails well, but pilot holes are essential for ease of working. Usually seen as a veneer, the wood is also used, solid, for knife handles, billiard cues, and in decorative areas where great resistance to handling is needed.

LACEWOOD
(exotic wood)

The version I've worked with, *Cardwellia sublimis*, is from Queensland, Australia, while another version, *Platanus acerafolia*, comes from Great Britain. The others are *Grevillea robusta*, from southern Australia, Africa, India and Sri Lanka (this stuff can give some people a rash much like they'd get from poison ivy), and *Panopsis rubescens* from Brazil. Lacewood in its Australian guise is also called silky oak, and in the British Isles version goes as planewood and harewood, as well as London plane, while *Panopsis* is also called leopard wood. Silky oak has a light-to-medium cherry background color that looks a lot like the rays exposed when white oak is quartersawn. The figure is consistent, with flaked silvery grain and large, regular medullary rays. Rays run at right angles to the axis of the tree, and are ribbons of tissue. They are called, interchangeably, medullary rays, pith rays and wood rays, as well as, simply, rays. The wood is medium weight, with straight grain except for the rays. Boards are unusually free of defects and knots. Texture is medium to coarse, and flat-sawn planks are apt to warp and cup. The cell walls surrounding the rays are prone to chipping out, so the wood must be cut carefully—use very, very sharp tools, and use backer boards wherever possible. With routers, planers and similar tools take several light passes. Hand-applied stains blotch, but alcohol-based spray stains work okay. The wood finishes well, holds nails and screws well and glues up nicely. I understand that it is considered an endangered species in Australia.

MAHOGANY, GENUINE
(exotic wood)

Many commercial woods are grouped under the name Mahogany. The original, *Swietenia*, came from the West Indies, and was the premier wood for fine furniture in Europe in the 1600s. American mahogany is sometimes, thus, referred to as genuine mahogany, while a related African wood, *Khaya*, is marketed as African mahogany. Stability is excellent in both African and American mahogany, and so is workability, gluing ability, and holding of nails and screws, though pilot holes, as always in hardwoods, work best with the latter. For several centuries mahogany has set the standard for other furniture hardwoods, and for hardwoods in general in many ways, as it doesn't warp, cup, check or otherwise give problems, and works easily with any kind of sharp tool. And it is gorgeous when polished to a superb sheen. *Khaya* is less stable than *Swietania*, but only by a single percentage point (about 12 percent).

MAHOGANY, PHILIPPINE
(exotic wood)

Better known as lauan, Philippine mahoganies are found in three genrea: *Shorea; Parashorea; Pentacme.* (I'm not going into the fine differences of each type.) As a whole, the species have a coarser texture than American mahogany *(Swietenia)* or the African mahoganies *(Khaya)*, and do not have dark-colored deposits in the pores. All lauan species have axial resin ducts aligned in long tangential lines in the end surfaces of the wood, and sometimes the ducts contain white deposits visible to the naked eye. The wood, though, is not resinous. Species are not durable, and are highly dense. Strength and shrinkage properties compare favorably with oak, and all groups machine easily, except white meranti which has a high silica content. In the U.S., most lauan shows up as inexpensive plywood.

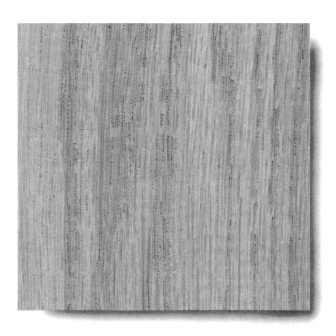

MAPLE, HARD
(hardwood)

OAK, RED
(hardwood)

Hard maple's texture is fine and very uniform, and the wood is medium heavy, strong, stiff, hard, resistant to shock, and has large shrinkage, though it's stable after seasoning. Usually, the grain is straight, with little figure, but different patterns, such as curly, fiddleback and bird's eye, add value to the wood in some applications. Hard maple can be hard to work because the grain variations create problems, as they do for stains, which may blotch. Rock maple also has a severe tendency to burn when sawn; extremely sharp tools and carbide-edged tools help prevent burning. It holds screws and nails well, without splintering, and also takes glue well. It finishes and polishes very well. Hard maples are medium to tall trees, usually topping out around 90 feet, with a trunk as much as 6 feet in diameter. Soft maple is lighter and weaker than hard maple, and is easier to work. Maple is especially useful for lumber, veneer and pulpwood, with much going into flooring, furniture, boxes, crates, shoe lasts, handles, woodenware, novelties, spools and similar turned items.

Quartersawn oak lumber is easily distinguished by the broad rays, which add to its good looks, and the rays are more evident in white oak. Red Oaks are generally found in the Southern States, the southern mountain regions, the Atlantic Coastal Plains and the Central States, and well up into southeastern Canada. Primary species are the Northern red oak *(Quercus rubra)*, scarlet oak *(Q. coccinea)*, Shumard oak *(Q. shumardii)*, pin oak *(Q. palustris)*, Nuttal oak *(Q. nuttallii)*, black oak *(Q. velutina)*, Southern red oak *(Q. falcata)*, water oak *(Q. nigra)*, laurel oak *(Q. laurifolia)* and willow oak *(Q. phellos)*. Northern red oak is a moderately fast-growing tree. Trees are medium-sized, reaching up to about 80 feet, with trunks as much as 5 feet in diameter. Red oak works well with hand and power tools, and doesn't require carbide-edged blades, but power tool woodworking is faster and easier with them. Red oak sapwood is nearly white, 1 or 2 inches thick, while heartwood is a reddish-brown, and coarse-grained. The open pores of red oak make it unsuitable for tightly sealed uses with liquids, without sealers or liners, but for the past couple of decades it has been the preferred wood for furniture. Oak glues well, holds screws and nails well if pilot holes are drilled — it has a tendency to split, a tendency emphasized by working close to wood edges — and it takes stains and finishes nicely. Much red oak goes into flooring, furniture, general millwork, boxes, woodenware and handles.

OAK, WHITE
(hardwood)

PADAUK
(exotic wood)

White Oaks are produced mostly in the South, South Atlantic and Central States, including the southern Appalachians. Principal species are white oak *(Quercus alba)*, chestnut oak *(Q. prinus)*, post oak *(Q. stellata)*, overcup oak *(Q. lyrata)*, swamp chestnut oak *(Q. michauxii)*, bur oak *(Q. macrocarpa)*, chinkapin oak *(Q. muehlenbergii)*, swamp white oak *(Q. bicolor)* and live oak *(Q. virginiana)*. *Q. alba* may stand as much as 115 feet tall, but almost never goes higher. Trunks may be 5 feet in diameter. Heartwood is grayish brown, and the sapwood, which may be 2 or more inches thick, is nearly white. White oak is a hard, tough, straight-grained wood, with even more of a tendency to splinter than that shown by red oak. It holds screws and nails well, if pilot holes are drilled, resists shock well and generally looks great. White oak figures are more attractive than red oak figures, and the wood is durable. White oak takes a good finish, with no filler required as it is in red oak, and glues easily with all woodworking adhesives, *except* epoxy. The presence of tannin—tannic acid—means you need to use stainless steel screws and nails, or brass, in outdoor projects to prevent the metals from being turned black. Never use soap to lubricate a screw or nail in white oak; the soap draws water and increases chances of problems. With white oaks in general, take shallow, multiple passes with planers, jointers and routers, and always use backing boards on cross-grain cuts to reduce splintering.

Often called barwood or camwood, and made up of seven species belonging to the genus *Pterocarpus*. African padauk, or *P. soyauxii*, is sometimes called vermillion, and is the only species most of us are likely to see today. The tree is moderate in height, topping out at no more than 100 feet, with a diameter, above the buttresses, of about a yard, or even 40 inches. The wood is hard and heavy, with interlocking grain and a moderately coarse texture. As with most interlocking-grain woods, quartersawing produces an attractive figure, this time a strong ribbon-stripe. Heartwood is a rich red-purple-brown with red streaks, and the sapwood is a pale beige (sapwood may also be as much as 8 inches thick). As it ages, the wood turns to a deep maroon. The wood works well with all tools, if they're sharp, takes glue well, and takes a fine finish. It holds nails and screws well, after pilot holes are drilled, and the heartwood is very durable. The wood must be dried slowly, but dries well, with moderate to low losses from distortion. It is a fine boatbuilding wood, and has been popular for top-grade furniture. It makes superb cutting board stock, too.

PINE, EASTERN WHITE
(softwood)

You can also find *Pinus strobus* under the names white pine, Northern white pine, Weymouth pine and soft pine. Eastern White Pine grows from Maine to northern Georgia, and over into the Lake States. The tree is of medium size, to 100 feet in height, and about 30 inches through the trunk. Heartwood is light brown, often tinged red, and turns considerably darker when exposed to light and air. The wood has reasonably uniform texture, and is straight-grained. It kiln dries easily, with little shrinkage, and ranks quite high in stability. It is also easy to work with all sharp tools, and is easily glued with almost all woodworking adhesives. Eastern white pine is lightweight, moderately soft, moderately low in strength, and has a low resistance to shock. Almost all this valuable resource is converted into lumber, and the number of items made from Eastern white pine is exceptionally wide; second-growth knotty lumber is used for containers and packaging, while high-grade lumber goes into casting patterns, sash, doors, furniture, trim, shade and map rollers, toys, and dairy and poultry supplies. Caskets and burial boxes also get their share. The wood works easily with conventional tools, but resin needs to be kept from building up. It is a good wood for carvers, and also takes finish well. Though it is relatively low in pitch, cleaning blades and bits frequently helps prevent burning. White pine is one of the lower cost woods and comes in many grades. On top of all that, it's the fastest growing tree in its range, often spurting up a foot and a half a year.

POPLAR, YELLOW
(hardwood)

A widely used, fast-growing, lightweight hardwood known as poplar, tulip poplar (that's the local name in my area) and tulipwood. Sapwood from yellow poplar is sometimes called whitewood or white poplar. The *Liriodendron tulipifera* range is great, running from New York and Connecticut down to Florida, and west to Missouri. The greatest commercial production is in the South and Southeast, and some of the largest logs in the area will be poplar. The tree is fast growing and reaches heights over 100 feet with frequency, often going to 165 feet. Shape is broadly conical, but the tree normally grows straight (though we've got one in the yard that leans a considerable bit), with branches starting well up the tree. Trunks reach to 6½ feet in diameter. Yellow poplar sapwood is white, and often several inches thick, while the heartwood is a yellowish brown, sometimes streaked with green, purple, black, blue or red. The wood is straight-grained and uniform in texture. Poplar works easily with hand and power tools, especially those that are kept sharp, and it glues up easily with all woodworking adhesives. It doesn't split easily, so it holds nails and screws well, but pilot holes are still a help when hand driving screws, or when within an inch of edges. Poplar takes stains, varnishes and paints well. Old-growth timber is lighter, weaker, lower in bending strength and softer, as well as lower in shock resistance, than newer growth. Lumber goes primarily into furniture, boxes, pallets, musical instruments, interior finish and siding.

PURPLEHEART
(exotic wood)

A maranth, or Purpleheart, comes out of the north central areas of the Brazilian Amazon region, though the species ranges from Mexico through Central America, and on down to southern Brazil. *Peltogyne spp.* comes from about 20 species of large trees, up to 150 feet, with logs over a yard in diameter, and is a dull brown when first cut. On exposure to air and light, the heartwood turns a deep purple, fading on prolonged exposure to light. Final wood tone is a rich red-brown. Textures vary across the different species, but are fine to moderately coarse; the grain is often interlocked, though it may also be straight. Quartersawing produces an attractive figure in logs with interlocked grain. Purpleheart is a heavy wood that dries slowly but well, with little loss due to distortion. It is a very strong wood and is stable in use, but difficult to saw. It is best cut and machined with carbide tools when power is used, as it dulls tools quickly because of its hardness. It is very durable, and finishes to a fine-looking gleam. It holds screws well, but demands pilot holes for easy working. The wood is resilient so splitting isn't a problem. It is also high in resin. It turns nicely and glues up well. Purpleheart stains nicely, too, though I can't imagine why anyone would stain it. The wood is used in turnery, fine furniture, cabinetry and carvings, but the largest use is in heavy construction because of its strength and durability.

ROSEWOOD
(exotic wood)

R osewoods are rare, highly decorative and highly prized members of the *Dalbergia* genus. Trees are small to medium in size, with the Indian rosewood tree *(Dalbergia latifolia)* reaching about 80 feet in height, while the Brazilian version, *Dalbergia nigra*, may reach 125 feet. Texture is uniform and moderately coarse, and the wood dries slowly but well. Indian rosewood has a subtle ribbon-grain figure because of interlocked narrow bands, and the color is a golden brown to a deep purple-brown, with streaks of dark purple or black. The wood is naturally durable, hard to work, easy to dry, and glues up best if mating surfaces are cleaned with a solvent such as alcohol. It dulls tools quickly, and only works anywhere near easily if tools are superbly sharp. Uses include musical instruments and veneers. Brazilian rosewood varies in color from rich brown to a dark violet-brown, with black streaks. The wood is oily, strong and steam bends well. The wood is also heavy, hard, moderately hard to work with hand tools, and keeps on resisting during power tool operations. The lumber contains calcareous (mineral) deposits, so it blunts tools quickly. Gum levels are also high enough to quickly create a mess on saw blades and sanding belts. Brazilian rosewood turns nicely, and has good screw-holding strength, though pilot holes are essential. Pores may need filling to get the smoothest surface. The wood is used for furniture, joinery, turning, carving and decorative veneers.

TEAK
(exotic wood)

TIGERWOOD
(exotic wood)

eavily grown in plantations throughout its natural range, and into Latin America and Africa, *Tectona grandis* is a tree of variable size, and may reach 125 feet when well grown, with a trunk nearly 6 feet in diameter. Wood texture is coarse and uneven, and teak has an oily feel. Grain may be straight or wavy. Burma teak tends to be uniform golden brown, while teak from other areas is a darker brown, with more black markings. Teak is strong, with good steam-bending qualities, and is very durable. There is a marked growth-ring figure on flat-sawn surfaces. The wood is heavier than mahogany, but not so heavy as oak, and is stable. It is about on a par with the oaks for strength. Teak works reasonably well, but the silica in the wood dulls tools quickly, so carbide edges are helpful. Teak glues and finishes well, if pretreatment is carried out in both cases. To get a good bond, clean all mating surfaces with alcohol or lacquer thinner, and give the entire piece a good wipe-down with thinner before applying a finish. The wood holds nails and screws well, but pilot holes are needed for ease of working. Teak does not cause rust or corrosion in contact with metals, so it has a field of use not open to other woods—for tanks and vats that must resist acids. Teak is a costly wood used in the construction of expensive boats, lawn furniture, flooring, decorative objects and decorative plywood.

Known outside the United States as African walnut (except in Africa where it is called Alonawood, Benin walnut, Congowood, Lovoawood and Nigerian golden walnut), Tigerwood, or lovoa (*Lovoa klaineana*) is a lovely, striped wood. The tree is large enough to produce logs four feet in diameter and two dozen feet long. The color is a pleasing bronze yellow-brown hue. The wood shows occasional dark stripes, from whence comes the name tigerwood. There is a ribbon stripe figure in quartersawn tigerwood, which more closely resembles mahogany than any of the true walnuts (*Juglans*). Tigerwood seasons well, and is stable when seasoned. It glues up nicely and machines well while taking an excellent finish whether being scraped or sanded. It ripsaws easily and cleanly, but is weaker than American black walnut. It also tears during turning if tools used aren't especially sharp—the same is true for drilling: Drill bits must be right up to a perfect edge or the holes are going to be ragged. This wood is a fine candidate for carbide-tipped brad point drill bits, and carefully maintained Forstner bits. Uses include decorative timbering, furniture making, paneling and veneering. It sometimes is stained and used to take the place of mahogany, and for gunstocks and inlays. Prefer it for cabinetry, furniture and inlays, since strength is a bit below the walnut standard for gunstocks.

WALNUT
(hardwood)

ZEBRAWOOD
(exotic wood)

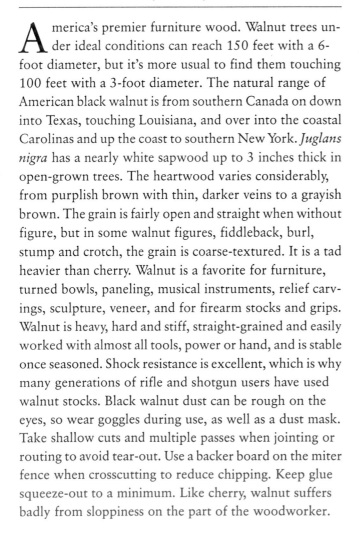

America's premier furniture wood. Walnut trees under ideal conditions can reach 150 feet with a 6-foot diameter, but it's more usual to find them touching 100 feet with a 3-foot diameter. The natural range of American black walnut is from southern Canada on down into Texas, touching Louisiana, and over into the coastal Carolinas and up the coast to southern New York. *Juglans nigra* has a nearly white sapwood up to 3 inches thick in open-grown trees. The heartwood varies considerably, from purplish brown with thin, darker veins to a grayish brown. The grain is fairly open and straight when without figure, but in some walnut figures, fiddleback, burl, stump and crotch, the grain is coarse-textured. It is a tad heavier than cherry. Walnut is a favorite for furniture, turned bowls, paneling, musical instruments, relief carvings, sculpture, veneer, and for firearm stocks and grips. Walnut is heavy, hard and stiff, straight-grained and easily worked with almost all tools, power or hand, and is stable once seasoned. Shock resistance is excellent, which is why many generations of rifle and shotgun users have used walnut stocks. Black walnut dust can be rough on the eyes, so wear goggles during use, as well as a dust mask. Take shallow cuts and multiple passes when jointing or routing to avoid tear-out. Use a backer board on the miter fence when crosscutting to reduce chipping. Keep glue squeeze-out to a minimum. Like cherry, walnut suffers badly from sloppiness on the part of the woodworker.

Also called zebrano and zingana, zebrawood is of the genus *Microberlinia brazzavillensis* (and also *M. bisculta*). The markings give it its name, with black longitudinal stripes on a light background. There are other species also known as zebrawood. The trees are large in size (both species), and tend to be inaccessible on and around the west coast of Africa, and at least until recently, harvesting was hazardous and expensive. Most often, zebrawood is used as a contrasting wood, with other woods serving as the main part of a project. The figure is in the heartwood, with the sapwood being almost featureless. Cross breaks occur on occasion, and are believed to be brought on by chemical changes as the tree grows. The drying is slow and difficult — the wood tends to twist, and is much better used quartersawn. Once dry, the wood is stable, in modest cross-sections. Grain is wavy and interlocked, and the wood is heavy and hard, and takes a fine polish with enough work. Quartersawn heartwood is a light gold in color, showing narrow streaks of exceptionally dark brown, or black, against the lighter colored background. The coarse texture of the wood demands great care in planing. The interlocking grain combined with coarse texture create a wood that tears if tools are not extremely sharp. Shock resistance is excellent, and it might well make attractive brush backs and tool handles, and possibly mirror handles, and similar items. Most is used as a veneer, where it tends to fragility before being glued to its substrate.

Chapter Three

NORTH AMERICAN HARDWOODS

Hardwoods are the furniture woods of the world and, as such, are classed as greater beauties than softwoods, while also being generally considered more costly and more difficult to work than softwoods. The woods listed here are domestic hardwoods of species you'd almost have to go way out of your way to avoid using if you're at all serious about woodworking. There are numerous others that are difficult to locate on a national basis, but one of the greatest things about being ready to prepare your own wood is the chance you have to pick up both bargains and unusual wood varieties. The working needs of most common United States and Canadian hardwoods are here, and, as with softwoods, there is enough detail to help you decide what to work with, how to work it, and how to care for it, but not so many particulars you'll be forever reading something that doesn't much matter in the day-to-day bustle of your shop, whether home or business. Nowhere do you learn all about every domestic hardwood. I don't know everything about every domestic hardwood, and, from the research I've done, I doubt anyone else does either. But you'll get what you need right here.

Alder, Red, is a Pacific Coast species used commercially in Washington and Oregon, where it is the most abundant commercial hardwood species. *Alnus rubra* has no visible boundary between heartwood and sapwood, with wood that varies from almost white to a pale, pinkish brown. Red alder is our largest domestic alder, sometimes reaching heights a bit over 80 feet, and ranging over 130 feet in rare instances. Growth is in the lowlands, and usually within 50 miles of saltwater. Tree growth is rapid, and tree life is short at 60 to 80 years. Alders provide shade and protection for longer-lived growth that comes after them. Too, the red alder has nitrogen-fixing nodules on the roots, so improves soil in much the same manner as does alfalfa. The wood is moderately light in weight, intermediate in most strength characteristics, and low in shock resistance. Alder rotary peels well to make veneer. Shrinkage during drying is relatively low. The wood is not durable. Red alder is principally used for furniture, doors, panel stock and millwork, and with its straight grain it makes a good carving wood. It requires sharp tools, whether hand or power, but is relatively easy to work. Unlike some hardwoods, alder doesn't insist the woodworker show up with carbide-tipped tools, though they help. It is exceptionally good for toys and similar projects, and has been used to make artificial limbs.

Apple is one of those woods that, if requested, will often bring a puzzled look to a commercial wood dealer's face. *Malus sylvestris* is available on a local and infrequent basis, and is also a good wood to mill yourself. Apple is not a commercial wood, but is grown, or is found, in most of North America. Check out local orchards to see if they are getting ready to take out old trees, and check local homeowners to see if they might be considering removing a nonproducing apple tree. The tree is small, seldom over 30 feet, and the trunk diameters vary wildly, and widely. The tree is often not shaped well, and trunks are often misshapen. Misshapen trunks produce distorted wood. Apple is a pale to medium pinkish brown in color, and has a fine, even texture. The wood weighs about the same as beech, and is hard to dry, when it tends to warp badly and split. It is slow drying and cannot be rushed, but is stable once dried. The wood is hard and strong. It saws and machines well with sharp tools, but getting a good finish, which can be done, is a lot of work. Irregular grain can tear out. It is not durable.

Apple is a good turning wood, and accepts fine detail and holds it, making it good for carving. It is often used for wooden screws, saw handles and as a decorative inlay, and is a superb wood for building small boxes.

Ash. See "Gallery of Wood."

Aspen consists of two species, bigtooth aspen *(Populus grandidentata)* and quaking aspen *(P. tremuloides)* that are mainly cut in the Northeastern and Lake States, with some production in the Rocky Mountain States. Also called "popple" and poplar, aspen is sometimes confused with tulip poplar (yellow poplar). Trees seldom exceed 60 feet in height and diameters don't go much beyond 20 inches. The wood resists splitting during nailing and works easily with hand tools. Sharp tools are necessary because the wood fibers tend to fuzz when worked. Apply a sealer before staining or the stain will blotch. Otherwise, the wood finishes well. Glues work well on aspen. It is not durable, but wears well indoors without splintering. Heartwood is gray-white to light gray-brown, with lighter colored sapwood that merges gradually into the heartwood without a clear defining line. The wood is straight-grained, with a fine uniform texture, and is easily worked with conventional tools. If properly seasoned, aspen will not impart flavor to foodstuffs. Lightweight and soft, aspen wood is also low in strength, moderately stiff, moderately low in resistance to shock, and has a moderately high rate of shrinkage during seasoning. Uses include toothpicks, boxes, crates, paneling and chipboard, pulpwood and veneer, as well as a range of turned articles. For woodworking

purposes, it is great for many projects, especially turned items, and it is a fine substitute for basswood when carving. It makes good toys because it almost never splinters. Cost is low, though in the South—sigh—it is hard to find. Next to impossible.

Basswood. See "Gallery of Wood."

Beech. See "Gallery of Wood."

Birch. See "Gallery of Wood."

Butternut. See "Gallery of Wood."

Catalpa, Northern and Southern, differ considerably in size. *Catalpa speciosa Warder* is the Northern version and is a medium tree topping out at about 95 feet, with a trunk as much as 40 inches in diameter. *Catalpa bignonioides Walt* is a small tree, seldom reaching 45 feet, but still sporting a 40-inch-diameter trunk on occasion. Both started originally with limited ranges, but have spread into coverage of most of the eastern United States through planting and escape into the wild from decorative plantings. Generally, the wood is scarce because this isn't a forest tree, and plantings are numerically small, with one or two trees reaching a mill at any one time. It is ring-porous, giving a bold figure to the grain, and resembles a darker chestnut wood. It tends to be splintery, fraying a bit when crosscut, something easily avoided by using super-sharp tools. Catalpa is durable, and has a strong aroma when cut, something of a musty spice odor. It is soft and open-grained, so needs to be protected against friction wear, as do woods like butternut and tulip poplar. Catalpa is useful for carving, and dries well without excess care

though it does take a long time. Shrinkage is relatively low, and the wood is stable after seasoning. It also glues up nicely, and there is little light-colored sapwood to spoil the darker heartwood. The wood finishes well, stains moderately well, and holds screws and nails securely. Drill pilot holes to prevent splitting. This is a more or less locally available wood, though over a wide area, and one you may be able to search out in some neighbor's yard, as it outgrows its space. The effort can be well worthwhile.

Cherry. See "Gallery of Wood."

Chestnut, American, once grew in vast commercial quantities from New England to northern Georgia. Almost all *Castanea dentata* has been killed by a blight introduced early in this century, and current supplies come from standing dead timber. This was once the dominant tree in the deciduous forest of eastern North America. Chestnut is so hardy that stumps continue to send up sprouts for decades after the main tree dies, with saplings often reaching 12 to 20 feet. Once the saplings start to mature, the blight knocks them off. The trees were once up to 115 feet tall, but mostly around 70 or 80 feet, with trunks up to 5 feet in diameter. Natural resistance to decay is incredible in this coarse-grained wood. Heartwood of chestnut is a gray-brown to brown, and darkens with age. Sapwood is very narrow and almost white. The wood is coarsely textured, with conspicuous growth rings pointed up by several large rows of distinct pores at the start of each year's growth. Chestnut wood is moderately light in weight, moderately hard, moderately low in strength, moderately low in resistance to shock and low in stiffness. It seasons well, shrinking moderately or little and is easy to work with conventional and power tools. Once used for poles, railroad crossties, shingles, furniture, caskets, boxes, crates and core stock for plywood panels, it now appears most often as wormy chestnut for paneling and picture frames. When you can locate old chestnut lumber now, it costs dearly, as the most expensive of all domestic woods—nearly on a par with ebony, in fact. Currently there are many experiments that seem to be showing signs of introducing a species of what one might call "almost" American chestnuts that are blight resistant. Too, there is an attempt being made to locate the last standing, blight-resistant trees and to reproduce those. One can hope those experiments, or cloning, will provide our children or grandchildren a view of this marvelous tree that we've been denied.

Cottonwood consists of several species of the genus *Populus*, with the most important being Eastern cottonwood *(P. deltoides)*, known as Carolina poplar and whitewood; swamp cottonwood *(P. heterophylla)*, also called cottonwood, river cottonwood and swamp poplar; black poplar *(P. trichocarpa)*; and balsam poplar *(P. balsamifera)*. Eastern cottonwood and swamp cottonwood grow throughout the eastern half of the United States, although the first adult cottonwood trees I ever saw were in the desert southwest of Salt Lake City some years ago. Eastern cottonwoods are fast-growing (as much as 5 feet in a single year), short-lived trees, reaching about 120 to 160 feet in height

and as much as 6½ feet in diameter. Black cottonwood grows in the West Coast States, and in western Montana, northern Idaho and western Nevada, while balsam poplar grows from Alaska across Canada, and in the northern Great Lakes States. Black cottonwood is a majestic tree, sometimes reaching over 160 feet, with a trunk almost 5 feet in diameter. Cottonwoods were once the signposts for wagon masters looking for water, because they're always on water: Even my desert cottonwoods were situated on a creek in the desert. Heartwood of the four cottonwoods is gray-white to light brown, with a whitish sapwood that merges gradually with the heartwood. The wood is fairly uniform in texture, straight-grained and odorless when seasoned well. Eastern cottonwood is moderately low in bending and compressive strength, moderately stiff, fairly soft, and fairly low in its ability to resist shock. Black cottonwood is slightly below Eastern cottonwood in most strength properties, and cottonwoods generally shrink a moderately large amount when seasoning. After curing, the wood is stable, and nail- and screw-holding ability is very good. The wood works easily, as noted, and it accepts all glues nicely. A sanding sealer helps reduce fuzzing; cottonwood may fuzz up when worked, so exceptionally sharp tools are a big help. Cottonwood generally is okay to stain, but not great. Clear finishes are probably best, without stains, or, of course, paint. Principal uses are for veneer, pulpwood, lumber and fuel. Cottonwood also makes a fine carving wood, requiring the same effort as basswood, though it is heavier. It does not work well with fine detail.

Dogwood is found over much of North America. It is a small tree, seldom as tall as 35 feet, with trunk diameters under 5 inches in most cases. *Cornus spp.* wood is hard, heavy, and very fine in texture, and usually has a straight grain. I don't ever remember seeing dogwood advertised commercially, though I'm sure some places have a supply from time to time. It is another tree that needs to be scoped out by the alert woodworker, so that it can be added to the home seasoning pile. The wood is a pinkish white, sometimes shading into that color from a pale yellow. It is about 15 percent heavier than beech. Dogwood seasons well, but is a slow drier. It is noted for strength, particularly toughness and hardness, and is hard to machine because of its density. Working properties are good, and it takes a superbly smooth finish. Dogwood is not durable. The wood is often used for shuttles and spindles in the textile industry because it resists wear well, taking on a sheen but not eroding. It makes a good wood for small turning and other projects in the home shop.

Elm, American, is another species of wood that will bring tears to your eyes: It is seriously threatened, and in some areas nearly extinct because of two diseases, so most of what's sold as elm today is from other elms. Disease-resistant hybrids are showing some signs of success, so the spreading elm that provided so much lumber for this country may not be gone. It's not yet as bad a case as chestnut, but *Ulmus Americana* is in deep trouble. Dutch elm disease, a fungus, and phloem necrosis have killed hundreds of thousands of trees. Other useful elms found in the United States and Canada include slippery elm *(U. rubra)*, rock elm *(U. thomasii)*, winged elm *(U. alata)*, cedar elm *(U. crassifolia)* and September elm *(U. serotina)*. Each of these is known by a number of names, depending on the area of the country in which it is located: American elm is called white elm, water elm and gray elm; slippery elm converts to red elm; rock elm is cork elm or hickory elm; winged elm is called wahoo; and cedar elm becomes basket or red elm, while September elm is red elm. A forest-grown elm may reach 140 feet, making it a large tree, with a trunk about 3 feet in diameter, but sometimes as much as 10 feet. Slippery elm is a moderately fast-growing tree, with a life span of about 150 to 200 years. Elm sapwood is nearly white, and the heartwood is a light brown, often with a reddish tint. Hard elms and soft elms exist, with the hard elms being rock elm, winged elm, September elm and cedar elm. American elm and slippery elm are the soft elms. Hardness and softness are based on weight. Most elms are more easily worked with power tools, as the wood is strong, tough and coarse-textured as well as being moderately heavy. Grain is sometimes straight, but also often interlocks. Elm glues well, and stains and polishes nicely. It holds nails and screws solidly, too. Elms have superb steam-bending qualities, and even soft elm is moderately heavy, with high shock resistance. It also resists decay well, so is good for boatbuilding. Most elm comes from the Lake, Central and Southern States, and main uses are boxes, baskets, furniture, and in veneer, and for fruit, vegetable and cheese boxes. Elm is another wood that has no characteristic odor or taste when seasoned, making it ideal for food contact uses

such as cutting boards. Elm burls are used in fine furniture veneers, too. This is an under-used wood for woodworkers, and as such may prove to be a bargain in some areas.

Hickory, pecan includes bitternut hickory, or *Carya cordiformis*; pecan *(C. illinoensis)*; water hickory *(C. aquatica)*; and nutmeg hickory *(C. myristiciformis)*. Bitternut hickory is found through the eastern half of the United States, and into Canada, while pecan hickory grows from central Texas and Louisiana to Missouri and Indiana. Water hickory resides from Texas to South Carolina, and nutmeg hickory is usually found in Texas and Louisiana. Wood of the pecan hickory differs little from true hickory, with a fairly wide band of nearly white sapwood, and a darker, whitish heartwood. The wood is heavy and hard, and has a very large shrinkage during drying. Pecan hickory is used in tool and implement handles, and flooring. High-grade logs go for decorative veneer and paneling. **Hickory, True,** is included with pecan hickories because of similarities in the wood, and because you'll almost never find them differentiated at any retail level. True hickories cover most of the eastern half of North America, once you get below the absolute total frost areas. Most important species include the shagbark, or *Carya ovata*, which at one time was the only hickory I'd ever heard about—back when I thought the wood made excellent fuel and little else (that opinion has changed slightly, but only slightly, because hickory is a bear to season and a double bear to work); pignut *(C. glabra)*; shellbark *(C. laciniosa)*; and mockernut *(C. tomentosa)*. My experience with hickory is that it

splits and checks a lot when drying, to the point that home-seasoning of the wood probably isn't worthwhile. And it truly is a rough one on tools: Years and years ago, I cut down a standing hickory, dead and seasoned, and only a foot in diameter. Before it was reduced to firewood, I had to sharpen a new chain saw chain four times. That tree gave me less than a half cord of firewood! Hickory trees are medium to tall, often around 100 feet, with trunks seldom more than a yard in diameter. Pecans will go to 200 feet and over 8 feet in diameter, just to keep things from getting dull, and the others occur between those two extremes. Hickory holds screws and nails well—but you absolutely have to drill first, for both. It also glues reasonably well. Wood texture is coarse, and grain is usually straight, though wavy and other irregular graining does occur. Hickory looks somewhat like ash, but is much heavier and harder. It is dense, tough, shock-resisting and is not durable. It dulls tools quickly, and almost demands carbide-tipped blades. It can be stained nicely and finishes up nicely, if its ring porosity is taken into consideration. For all commercial uses, the greatest production of true hickory comes from the Central and Middle Atlantic States. The Southern and South Atlantic States produce nearly half of all hickory lumber. Sapwood is nearly white, and the heartwood tinges to the red, with both sapwood and heartwood weighing the same. True hickory is exceptionally hard, heavy and tough, strong, and shrinks a lot in seasoning. Tool handles use a lot of hickory, as do ladder rungs, poles and furniture. Of course, hickory also serves as a flavoring, going for charcoal and being used in meat packing houses to smoke meat. For the home workshop, use hickory where extreme toughness is needed. It's superb, for example, when used as chair rungs and rockers and it bends reasonably nicely with steam.

Holly is often considered a domestic exotic, probably because it tends to be both hard to find and costly. *Ilex opaca* price seems to run a buck or so above walnut, and you might find some mixed with soft maple—for far less money, of course—not too far south of southwest Virginia, where the trees reach their maximum sizes. The range is most of the eastern United States (from eastern Pennsylvania south and east to east Texas), and the tree is slow-growing and long-lived. Holly is difficult to dry, and best dried in small sizes. Even after drying, it is not dimensionally stable, producing a lot of movement as humidity changes, further reinforcing the need to work it in small sizes. Trees seldom exceed 45 feet, with a trunk 2 feet in diameter; most are considerably smaller. Holly is the whitest wood known, with pure white sapwood and a creamy heartwood and with little to distinguish between the two. It is moderate in weight, but hard enough to make working it difficult with hand tools. It glues up nicely and resists splitting, so it holds screws and nails well. It is fine-grained and sands to an extreme smoothness. Holly also accepts stain beautifully. It turns well, and is a good choice for carvers who use power tools or keep gouges super sharp.

Laurel, California, is a local wood, usually called Pacific myrtle and pepperwood (the leaves have a sharp, spicy aroma when bruised),

and has as a distant cousin the more widely available sassafras. *Umbellularia californica* is at home on the range between the mountains and the Pacific, reaching down from southern Oregon almost to Mexico's Baja peninsula. This coastal hardwood is an evergreen, and is not even a small tree but more of a large bush in much of its range, though in the best areas it may reach 80 feet tall with a 3½-foot trunk diameter. Laurel's sapwood is tan, and the heartwood is close-grained and a light brown. There is a pronounced figure in almost all cuts, and the wood produces many bird's-eye figures, mottles and swirls. The wood is hard, heavy and strong, comparing favorably to red oak in these characteristics, but is much tighter-grained and less apt to splinter than any oak. Laurel or myrtle makes a good turning wood, finishes nicely, but doesn't work well with hand tools. In fact, carbide edges are recommended, and even then you'll get some tear-out during planing and routing. Laurel glues nicely, takes screws and nails well, and is so tight-grained that sanding sealers aren't needed. It takes stain and all finishes well. Cost is on a par with cherry, unless you want to work burl veneers, when the cost goes up quickly. The lumber is hard to find.

Locust, Black, is a wood that is often overlooked for workshop purposes and relegated to the fence posts that keep sheep and goats away from the shop doors. *Robinia pseudoacacia* is found from Pennsylvania along the Appalachian Mountains down into northern Georgia and Alabama. It also is found west to Arkansas, and in southern Missouri. Most production comes out of my area, Virginia,

West Virginia, Tennessee and Kentucky. The tree is small, with a ropy looking bark, seldom exceeding 35 feet around here, though I've seen some that reached 55 feet. Diameters may reach almost 42 inches, but most of the ones I see are under 30 inches, often no more than 2 feet. Locust sapwood is narrow and creamy in color, and fresh-cut heartwood ranges from greenish yellow to dark brown. The wood darkens to a good-looking medium gold-brown. The wood is coarse textured and straight-grained, and weighs about the same as oak. Black locust is a very hard, very heavy wood with very high resistance to shock, and very high overall strength and stiffness. Moderately small shrinkage makes it reasonable for home seasoning, though it must be dried slowly to keep distortion to a minimum. Heartwood has a high decay resistance. The wood is fairly hard to machine, and much easier to work with carbide-tipped power tools. Shrinkage and swelling are both moderate, and it glues nicely and holds nails and screws snugly. It also bends well, and takes a decent finish without excess work, though it's ring porous and requires filler for smoothest results. I've never tried staining it, but it is said to stain and take finishes well. Today, most locust is destined for use as fence posts, rails, crossties and fuel. At one time, it was used as treenails in ships, and for a much wider variety of chores, most of which may be replicated in the modern wood shop.

Magnolia (Southern, sweetbay and cucumber tree), comprise a group of trees that are classed as magnolia for lumber purposes. *Magnolia grandiflora* (Southern), *M. vir-*

giniana (sweetbay or swamp magnolia) and *M. acuminata* (cucumber tree) have an extended Southern United States range, all the way up into Ohio and southern New York, but Louisiana leads in production of magnolia lumber. Sapwood of the Southern magnolia is yellowish-white, and heartwood a light to dark brown, tinged with yellow or green. The wood has a close, uniform texture, and is straight-grained, closely resembling tulip poplar (in appearance). It turns nicely, and steam bends well, too. Magnolia is another wood with no characteristic odor or taste, so it is superb for turned bowls. Around where I live, you find a lot of gouged wood dough bowls made from cucumber tree wood: A dough bowl is used for kneading dough that's to rise, and can be made of many woods, but preferably those with no taste or odor to impart to the bread or rolls. Magnolia takes finishes nicely and stains well. It glues up well and doesn't split easily when nails or screws are used. Wood is moderately heavy, moderately low in compressive and bending strength, and moderately hard, stiff, and high in shock resistance. Principal uses are in making furniture, boxes, sash, doors and veneers, and in general millwork. Magnolia is an often ignored wood that costs about the same as poplar, and is at least as useful. It is readily available throughout its range, and may sometimes be mistaken for soft maple.

Maple, Hard. See "Gallery of Wood."

Maple, sugar and soft, are the major divisions one should expect when buying maple in the United States and Canada. There's a lot of additional definition of species, but *Acer saccharum* and black maple *(A. nigrum)* are hard maple, and all else is softer maple, to me not nearly as useful or as much fun to work. Still, silver maple *(A. saccharinum)*, red maple *(A. rubrum)*, box elder *(A. negundo)* and bigleaf maple *(A. macrophyllum)* provide woods excellent within their own limits. Sugar maple, though, known also as hard or rock maple, is the maple of bowling pins, bowling alley lanes, and other uses where extreme shock resistance, resistance to abrasion, good looks and easy upkeep are essential. Maple lumber production is primarily from the Middle Atlantic States and the Lake States. We see a few maples here in Virginia, but generally, the hard maples are found from Indiana and Wisconsin east, dipping down into Tennessee, but swinging up along the Appalachians, hanging around mostly on the western mountain slopes. Softer maples grow almost everywhere, in one variety or another. Maple sapwood is commonly white and as much as 5 inches thick, with heartwood a light, reddish brown.

Mesquite brings to mind tumbling tumbleweeds and a charcoal grill or smoker, but it is also an excellent choice for woodworking of several kinds. Three varieties of mesquite *(Prosopis glandulosa, P. juliflora* and *P. pubsecens)* provide wood for carvings, turnings and furniture. Mesquite grows to about 50 feet tall as a maximum, with a trunk that may reach 3 feet in diameter. There won't be a lot of straight wood in that trunk as it twists and turns its way upward, but the mesquite wood has a lovely tightly interlocking grain with a narrow tan sapwood bordering deep brown heartwood. Mesquite has a limited range, but covers a lot of ground within that range: It covers 75 million acres in Texas alone, and extends down into Mexico, and into Oklahoma and Arizona, becoming a sturdy shrub in desert areas. During seasoning, shrinkage occurs evenly, so mesquite remains almost unusually stable; it may be carved green as there will be no checking as it dries. You need power tools for this heavier-than-oak wood that also has a high silica content—which means you also need carbide-edged tools to retain cutting edges for long. The wood is also brittle, so, with the silica content, you need to use screws and glue for joinery. Wipe down surfaces with alcohol or lacquer thinner before gluing. You can get a superb, fine finish and it takes clear finishes well. Stains are not necessary. Mesquite is great for small to medium turnings and for carving. It is moderate in price, though top-grade stock can cost double the price of walnut.

Oak, Red. See "Gallery of Wood."

Oak, White. See "Gallery of Wood."

Pear is another fruitwood that generally is widely available, mostly from wood from old orchard trees, as is apple wood. *Pyrus communis* is a small tree, seldom over 35 feet, though a few may reach 55 feet. The wood is a pale pink-brown, with a very fine texture—finer than apple's texture. The grain is straight if the stem bearing the wood is straight, irregular otherwise. It weighs about the same as beech. It dries slowly, with a tendency to distort, and if the grain is irregular, it distorts even more; dry very, very slowly. Pear wood is strong, tough and difficult to split. It is fairly hard to saw, and is rough on tool edges, so carbide blades are best. It is not durable. Pear takes a fine finish, and reacts well to most glues. Small sizes are available, and you may need to search the wood out by checking local orchardists to see if they have, or know someone who has, old trees to be taken down. The wood is used for drawing instruments, T squares and in cabinetwork.

Persimmon is another backyard tree that provides woodworkers with some unique qualities (including an invasion of the lawn with sprouts once the trees are established). *Diospyros virginiana* is of the same family as ebony, and is, in fact, sometimes called white ebony. The tree is usually found in the South, but occurs on up into New York and Connecticut. The trees are fairly slow growing, and the fruit, after it ripens properly, is choice. You must wait until the skin wrinkles and the fruit gets mushy. If you don't wait, expect to spend two days puckered up as if you had sucked a barrel of lemons; firm persimmons are incredibly bitter. The tree is small, not over 65 feet tall most of the time, with a trunk to 30 inches in diameter. The wood is off-white with a gray-brown tint, heavy, and of little commercial use because the lumber it provides is not very good. Wood texture is fine, and grain is straight. The wood is dense, about 15 percent heavier than beech, but not nearly as dense as black ebony. Persimmon dries with fair ease, but shrinks a great deal. Even when dry, it moves a lot under changing humidity. It works well with power tools, and can be worked with hand tools. Carbide-edged tools are rec-

ommended for power working with persimmon. Strength qualities exceed those of beech, and the wood takes an excellent finish and wears well. In the textile industry, shuttles may be made from persimmon, and it is traditionally used in golf club heads because of its exceptional hardness. Impact resistance is also exceptional.

Poplar, Yellow. See "Gallery of Wood."

Sassafras is probably better known for its qualities as a beverage than as a furniture-quality wood. *Sassafras albidum* covers a great deal of the eastern half of the United States, and resembles black ash (a most useful and lovely ash) in color, grain and texture. Trees range from small to moderately large depending on growing conditions, with the usual tree a medium size, reaching no more than 50 feet tall, with a 40-inch-diameter trunk. The trees are long-lived, though, and may live a millennium, during which time they'll attain a height over 100 feet and a diameter of about 5 feet. Sassafras works easily with hand tools, but planing has a tendency to lift the grain if edges aren't kept very sharp. It glues well, sands easily, and takes a fine finish. Drill pilot holes for screws and nails. Sassafras sapwood is light yellow, while heartwood ranges from dull gray to brown and dark brown, occasionally with a red tinge. The wood is moderately light for a hardwood, weak in bending and endwise compression, soft, brittle, very high in shock resistance, and durable in the weather. It is not useful where weight must be borne, but it is a good carving wood and a good turning wood with unusual grain

patterns. Most use is local, for fence posts and general millwork. The roots with their oil of sassafras are used to make tea, perfume and soaps and were once used as a patent medicine. The small amount of oils in the wood gives it a characteristic odor: To check what you're getting, run a scraper over the wood. It is aromatic, with a medicinal odor that is mild enough to be quite pleasant.

Sweetgum ranges from southern Connecticut west to Missouri and south to the Gulf, but lumber production is almost entirely from Southern and South Atlantic States. Sweetgum trees are among the loveliest fast-growing hardwoods—something of a surprise to me, as I had always thought they were slow-growing, and planted one with that premise about five years ago. Whoops. Yard space is disappearing more quickly than I expected. Eventual *Liquidambar styraciflua* size may be as much as 130 feet, with a 4-foot-diameter trunk and a great-looking pyramid shape. Fall colors are spectacular, ranging from orange to red—on the same tree. Sapwood and heartwood are solidly differentiated to the point where each is classed as a different wood: Sapgum is the light-colored sapwood, redgum is the red-brown heartwood. Don't fool with the sapgum. The following features are for redgum, or heartwood sweetgum, only. Sweetgum, like tupelo (black gum), has interlocking grain, which makes it very useful for some woodworking applications, and a pure horror for anything that requires splitting or similar operations. Your tools must be exceptionally sharp to do well, especially when you're turning this wood. Wipe wood with alcohol—all faces—before gluing. It holds screws and nails very well, and is not subject to excessive splitting once dry. Drying must be undertaken carefully and slowly and without extreme changes, but it can be successfully home-dried, with moderate losses to warp and cupping. Distortion will be extreme if you rush it. Quartersawn sweetgum with interlocked grain produces a lovely ribbon-stripe figure that is superb in many furniture uses. Sweetgum takes finishes well and comes up to a truly lovely luster. The wood is moderately heavy and hard. It is fairly strong, stiff, and high in shock resistance. Mainly used for lumber, veneer, plywood and pulpwood, sweetgum goes into boxes, furniture, interior trim and millwork.

Sycamore, American, is sometimes called the buttonwood tree and the plane tree. It grows from Maine west to Nebraska and south to Texas, thence on east to Florida. The Central States produce the most *Platanus occidentalis* lumber. Sycamores are large trees, often to 125 feet and more than 10 feet in diameter. They grow rapidly in bottomlands that are well wetted, often reaching 80 feet at 20 years. Sycamore heartwood is reddish brown, with lighter-colored sapwood from 1½ to 3 inches thick. The wood is finely textured, with even, interlocking grain. Sharp tools reduce tear-out. Sycamore glues well and finishes well. It shrinks moderately in drying, and is moderately heavy, moderately stiff, moderately strong, and has good resistance to shock. Quartersawn stock seasons easily, but plainsawn sycamore will warp and cup a lot. The wood has no characteristic odor or taste, so it makes good containers and utensils

for food. It is not durable. Sycamore handles a lot like cherry—fast feed, light cuts, several passes, sharp tools—but it has more of a tendency to burn, as if it were maple. Sycamore sands without effort and takes a glasslike finish. All adhesives perform well, and the wood resists splitting, so pilot holes are only essential when you're hand driving screws. Plainsawn sycamore takes stain well, but quartersawn stock must be tested to see if a particular stain works properly. It's best to apply a sealer. Sycamore carves easily and well, and is a fine turning wood, too. Sycamore primarily makes furniture, flooring, handles and butcher blocks, and the veneer is used for fruit and vegetable baskets.

Tupelo has a bunch of names for several species: water tupelo *(Nyssa aquatica)*, also called swamp tupelo and tupelo gum; black tupelo *(N. sylvatica)*, known also as black gum and sourgum; and several other variants. The main variants are tall trees, ranging up to and over 100 feet with a 3-foot-diameter trunk. Tupelo dries easily enough but has a tendency to distort a lot, so slow and careful procedures are essential. It is resistant to splitting, so nails and screws hold well, even without pilot holes. All, except for black gum, grow primarily in the southeastern United States; black gum grows from Maine down to Texas and Missouri. About two-thirds of tupelo lumber comes from the Southern States. Wood of the different tupelos is similar in appearance and properties. Heartwood is a light brown, casting to gray, and merges gradually into the lighter-colored sapwood. The sapwood is several inches wide. Tupelo wood has a fine, uniform texture and an inter-

locked grain. It can be hard to work because of the interlocked grain, and may also be difficult to finish. Use carbide tools whenever possible. Feed boards at a slight angle during planing, and use a slow feed when ripping. Too fast a feed causes burning of edges with tupelo. Take several light passes when jointing or routing, and use slow drilling speeds. Tupelo glues up well, if surfaces are smooth, and it takes all stains and finishes nicely. It is a good carving wood, but not a particularly good turning wood. Tupelo is not durable. It rates as moderately heavy, moderately strong, moderately hard and stiff, and moderately high in shock resistance, making it suitable for many uses. Main uses are lumber, veneer and pulpwood.

Walnut. See "Gallery of Wood."

Willow, Black, is the only willow commercially handled under its own name. *Salix nigra* is produced mainly in the Mississippi Valley, from Louisiana to southern Missouri and Illinois. Usually a small- to medium-sized tree, the black may reach 60 feet in the North, but on good sites in the South, expect willows to attain 120 feet and more. Trunks will range from 2 feet to 6½ feet in diameter. Black willow may grow 50 feet in its first 10 years of life, but is a short-lived tree that probably won't see 100 years. Black willow heartwood is gray-brown or a light red-brown, with darker streaks often found. Sapwood is a whitish, creamy yellow. Grain is interlocked, though not as tightly as with tupelo and sweetgum, and the wood is finely textured. Willow is light in weight, low in strength—very much so as a beam or post—and is moderately soft, with fairly high shock resistance. The wood tends to be light and springy, thus the popularity of willow baskets and wickerwork furniture. Shrinkage during drying is moderately large, but once dry, willow is stable. It is not durable. Willow works well with all tools, power and hand, but favors those who bring sharp tools to the work at hand. It accepts glues readily and takes finishes well. Willow principally makes lumber, but small amounts go for veneer, cooperage, pulpwood, artificial limbs and fence posts.

Chapter Four

EXOTIC HARDWOODS AND SOFTWOODS

When I started this chapter, my intent was to sort of glide over a few of the less exotic woods. I had decided not to cover woods that are extremely expensive and usually hard to obtain in any kind of rough state that allows saving much money over retail prices. Then, of course, I began to find old favorites, often woods that haven't seen shop light in years, and I realized that exotic woods are just as much joy to work. So you'll find more exotic woods listed than I originally planned to cover. I expect the listings to help, because they provide information on woods you may not meet with great frequency.

Exotic woods tend to have more strongly figured, often gaudy appearances, and to accentuate features some of our domestic woods have only slightly. For example, only mesquite has enough silicon to create problems, while teak is murder on tools because of its silicon load and doesn't glue easily, but it lasts like stainless steel (that latter is only a very slight exaggeration). Many exotic woods are resistant to weathering, but most are so costly only small projects are built from them: If you can afford a teak or avodire deck, you are one unusual woodworker!

I've tried to list as many names as possible for each of the various species, because many have several verbal variants that may not be well known. However, angelique and avodire are exceptions, and there are many others with single names.

I am not going to get into deforestation, ruination of the rain forests and similar subjects: First, there is too much conflicting evidence; second, until emotions are allowed to run more quietly, there will be little progress made in dealing with these matters. The only so-called fact that appears reasonable is that the residents of the areas being deforested seem to have a habit of burning forests to clear land for farming. That is in no way affected by harvesting wood for lumber users, and is not something woodworkers, as woodworkers, have any power to control. Thus, to our exotic woods:

African blackwood is a relative of the rosewoods, and is a lovely wood, if very costly, in its own right. *Dalbergia melanoxylon* comes from a small, usually misshapen tree, with supplies mainly available from Mozambique and Tanzania. The wood is characteristically black, and is shipped only in short billets. It is a rare wood, and the price is on a par with Brazilian rosewood, which is also rare. African blackwood is dark purple-brown to black, has a fine, even texture, and a straight to irregular grain. It is exceptionally heavy, barely lighter than lignum vitae, and slightly oily to the touch. It is hard to dry but is very slow to change moisture content once dry. It tends to brittleness, so care is needed in machining—very sharp tools, light cuts. African blackwood is primarily used for woodwind music instruments, such as oboes, flutes and clarinets, and for the chanters of bagpipes. It is used for turned items and African carvings as well, and is hard to glue. It holds screws particularly well, and is stable enough, and strong enough to be threaded to take machine screws.

Amaranth (see *Purpleheart*).

Andiroba is a widespread wood in tropical America, and also goes under the names of cedro macho, carapa, crabwood and tangare. *Carapa guianensis* is the primary, and best, source of andiroba wood, but *C. nicaraguensis* is another and somewhat inferior wood that sells under the same name. Heartwood color varies from red-brown to dark red-brown, and the texture is like that of American mahogany *(Swietenia)*; the wood is sometimes used in place of mahogany. Grain is interlocked, but rates as easy to work, paint and glue. The wood is very durable, and is heavier than mahogany, as well as superior in bending properties, compression strength, hardness and toughness. For gluing, no special tricks are required. Andiroba makes excellent flooring, furniture and cabinetwork, millwork, veneer and plywood where durability and beauty must be combined.

Angelique comes from French Guiana and Surinam. The tree from which angelique comes is large, up to 160 feet, with logs as much as 2 feet in diameter. *Dicorynia guianensis* has heartwood that is russet-colored when fresh cut, turning to a dull brown, with a purple cast. Heartwood that stays more distinctly red often shows wide bands of purplish color. Texture is coarser than that of black walnut, and the grain may be straight or mildly interlocked. Angelique is stronger than teak and white oak, whether green or air dried. It is highly resistant to decay and to marine borers, but working qualities differ depending on degree of seasoning and silica content. Once completely dried, angelique is only workable with carbide-tipped power tools. Mating surfaces must be carefully cleaned with alcohol or lacquer thinner before gluing. It is most suitable for heavy structures, but may also serve in garden projects such as benches.

Avodire ranges from Sierra Leone west to the Congo, and south to Angola. It is most common on what was the Ivory Coast, and is scattered elsewhere. *Turraeanthus africana* forms a medium-sized tree of the rain forest. Wood is cream to a pale yellow in color, with a high natural luster. It eventually darkens to a golden yellow. The grain is straight on occasion, but is more often interlocking in a wavy or irregular pattern. The figure produced when quartersawn is unusually and attractively mottled. Avodire is identical in strength with oak, though considerably lighter (about 85 percent as heavy) and lower in shock resistance. It works reasonably easily with hand and power tools, and finishes well. It accepts most glues well, too. Most imported avodire is in the form of highly figured veneer, and is used in fine joinery, cabinetry, paneling and furniture.

Balsa is a wood with which all kids, or seemingly all, got experience back in the forties and fifties when model airplanes attained massive popularity, though they were exceptionally difficult for even a talented adult to construct. The wood works with exceptional ease, glues readily, sands easily and finishes nicely. *Ochroma pyramidale* is widely distributed throughout tropical America, from southern Mexico to southern Brazil and Bolivia, though Ecuador has been the primary source since balsa became economically important. Found at lower elevations, it is often cultivated in plantations today. Balsa is an exceptionally fast-growing wood, reaching its mature height of 70 feet and diameter of 2 feet within seven years. It is short-lived, seldom living more than fifteen years. It dries easily and is quite stable when dry. It is easily worked with sharp tools, hand or power. Several characteristics of balsa make a wide range of uses possible. It is the lightest and softest of all woods marketed, often weighing as little as 6 pounds per cubic foot when totally dry (most weighs around 11 pcf). Construction of the wood is very porous, trapping air and thereby adding to buoyancy, insulation against heat and cold, and absorption of sound. Balsa wood is easily recognizable by weight alone, but the wood is almost white, with an oatmeal texture that also makes it easy to tell from other woods. It may have a yellow or pink tint, and has a velvety feel. Principal uses are in life-saving gear such as rafts and life rings, core stock, insulation and models.

Boxwood is more of a European wood than American, but is not truly an exotic. Still, it's not domestic, so I'm placing *Buxus sempervirens* with the more costly, less readily available woods. The tree is small, seldom exceeding 35 feet, and not much more than 6 inches in diameter. It is found in Europe, Asia Minor and Western Asia. The wood is very fine, even-textured, hard, dense and heavy, and grain may be straight or irregular. It is so dense that even dried specimens barely float in water. When cut, boxwood is a pale yellow, but mellows to a yellow-tan. Boxwood splits badly if a careful check isn't kept on speed of drying—slowly does it best. With sharp tools, boxwood is easy to cut, and it makes a superb turning wood. Boxwood also is a good carver's wood when exceptional detail is needed. We often see it in folding measuring rules and in rulers. It glues up nicely and stains well. Boxwood also polishes to a fine finish.

Bubinga. See "Gallery of Wood."

Ceiba comes from the silk-cotton tree, the same tree that gives us kapok, used in mattresses and life vests, among other places. *Ceiba pentandra* occurs widely in the tropics, and sometimes is a huge tree, reaching 200 feet, with a trunk 6 feet in diameter being common. It ranges much of the Ivory Coast of West Africa, among other places, and *Ceiba samauma* is found in South America. The wood is pale and light in weight, lighter than obeche, but heavier than balsa. It is not as bright looking as those two, because the texture is coarser. Ceiba is difficult to handle and prone to fungus problems, but is exceptionally durable, resisting, after drying, both fungus and termite attack. Nail- and screw-holding characteristics are poor, and ceiba has a high percentage of tension wood— the reason it does not machine well. It is very stable once dried. Overseas quantities tend to be limited because of demands made in its home areas, but ceiba is used for boxes, joinery, furniture components and veneer, especially core veneers for other face varieties.

Cocobolo. See "Gallery of Wood."

Ebony. See "Gallery of Wood."

Goncalo alves. See "Gallery of Wood."

Greenheart is a wood from a medium to large tree, up to about 130 feet tall and 40 inches in diameter. *Ocotea rodiaei* is a pale yellowish green to dark olive-colored wood, sometimes with darker striations that are almost black. It is found in Guyana in commercial quantities. Texture is fine and even, while grain is interlocking, though it may also be straight. The wood is very dense, and will not float in water, even when dry. Greenheart is a slow drier with a tendency to check and split, but is exceptionally strong even for its weight: It is almost twice as strong as oak in bending, compression and stiffness! The wood is hard to work with all tools, virtually demanding sharp carbide blades, and the splinters can cause sepsis. It is resistant to almost every kind of insect, worm or fungus. Greenheart also resists abrasion well, and is often used in heavy construction. It makes good turnings, and is especially superb for any applications where you might need long, slender rods, such as in making fishing poles.

Jarrah is one of the Australian offerings to the world. This wood is also known as Australian Mahogany. *Eucalyptus marginata* has a small range, along the coast south of Perth, in Australia, but it is very common there. The tree is a modest size for a eucalyptus, seldom going over 150 feet (other eucalyptus species may reach heights of 200 feet). The heartwood is medium to dark brown after age and exposure take over, but freshly cut, it's a uniform pink to dark red, a rich mahogany color. Sapwood is pale in color and very narrow in older trees, wider in newer growth. Grain is often interlocked and wavy, and texture is even but moderately coarse. The wood glues satisfactorily, but drill pilot holes if nailing or driving screws—it tends to be splintery in some situations. Gum veins create some problems in this hard, heavy wood that rates as very resistant to termite attack. The wood is difficult to work by hand because of the high density and interlocking grain. Jarrah is often used for heavy construction, exterior and interior millwork, furniture, turnery and decorative veneers.

Jelutong comes out of Malaya, where it is also important in the production of the latex used in chewing gums. *Dyera costulata* is a tall tree, running up as much as 190 feet, with a straight-grained, nearly lusterless wood. Heartwood and sapwood are not differentiated, and the wood is straw-colored, fine textured, and has no distinctive figure. It weighs about the same as poplar, is not durable, and has a firm, soft texture. Jelutong dries quickly and well, with little distortion. It is stable in use when dry, and is a weak wood. It works well with sharp tools, either hand or power, and can be given a very smooth finish. Latex cavities create problems in getting large-size pieces of wood, so the good working properties and fine texture go mostly into handicraft work, toys and models where the wood's ability to hold fine detail when carved also stands it in good stead.

Kapur is found in Malaya, Sumatra and Borneo. *Dryobalanops spp.* is a tall tree, to 190 feet, with a long, straight trunk and a reddish brown heartwood clearly marked from the pale sapwood. The wood is uniform in texture, but fairly coarse, and is straight-grained. The wood is a little heavier than oak, and is suitable for outdoor projects in particular, as it is stable and durable once dried. It is moderately heavy, and the heartwood is resistant to decay. It works with moderate ease with hand and power tools, but is best machined with carbide-tipped tools because it has a high silica content which blunts edges quickly. Dull cutters also tend to raise the grain rather badly. Kapur takes nails and screws well, after pilot holes are drilled, but it is not easily bonded with adhesives. Use urea formaldehyde adhesives for best results.

Kingwood is another of the *Dalbergia* species, this time *Dalbergia cearensis*, and the wood is often called violet wood or violetta. The tree is small, related to rosewood, and produces short logs, usually 8 feet and under, with a diameter of no more than 8 inches once sapwood is removed. The wood is finely textured and even, heavy and lustrous. Heartwood has a variegated striped figure of violet and black on brownish purple. Sapwood is white. The wood is hard and heavy, but works well with sharp tools, and takes a fine polish. It glues well. Most uses are for inlays, turnery and marquetry.

Koa is Hawaii's contribution to the exotics. Since it is a U.S. wood, maybe it should be listed as a domestic hardwood, but *Acacia koa* grows in quantity only in the Hawaiian Islands, where it seems to grow just about everywhere. The mature trees reach 120 feet with 8-foot-diameter trunks, and, in stands, may be free of branches for 80 feet. Koa weighs about 50 percent more than black walnut, and has similar high shock-absorbing qualities. Koa, though, has interlocking grain, so that a superb fiddleback figure shows up with some frequency. The sapwood is light-colored, and the heartwood is primarily red-brown, going to dark brown, sometimes with tones of gold, black and deep purple. Bending strength is great, and the wood works well with conventional hand and power tools, though it may burn during routing or crosscutting. It is best planed at a slight angle, with a fast feed, to keep the grain from tearing. Koa is best joined with screws as

well as glue because there are resin pockets that sometimes prevent good gluing. Koa sands to a truly superb, silky look. Uses include gunstocks, veneers, paneling, boat trim—it is decay resistant—furniture, sculpture and general turnings. Cost is about a dollar or so a board foot more than walnut, grade for grade.

Lacewood. See "Gallery of Wood."

Lignum vitae is one of the woods you'll seldom if ever work with, but you may have it around the shop in the form of tools: The best mallet I ever had was made of this waxy, supremely heavy wood (it not only doesn't float, it sinks fairly quickly). Current supplies are mostly *Guaiacum santcum*, and are found in the West Indies, northern Venezuela, northern Colombia, Panama and into southern Mexico. It is one of the heaviest and hardest woods on the market with a waxy feel, and a fine, uniform texture and tightly interlocked grain. The wood is a characteristic green color. There is absolutely no way to mistake lignum vitae for any other wood. The resin content may make up a quarter of the air-dry weight of the heartwood. The waxy resin gives the wood a self-lubricating property that makes it nearly ideal for pulley blocks, caster wheels, turned articles and brush backs.

Limba is also called ofram and afara. It is widely distributed from Sierra Leone to Angola and Zaire, and is favored as a plantation tree in West Africa. It reaches moderately large sizes, close to 140 feet, with a possible 40-inch-thick trunk. Heartwood in *Terminalia superba* varies from

gray-white to creamy or yellowish brown, with frequent almost black streaks. The resulting figure is highly prized for decorative veneers. The wood is straight-grained and uniform, but coarse, in texture. Strength is moderate, and some timber may be brittle. Limba seasons easily with slight shrinkage, and is easy to work with hand and power tools. It peels for veneering without problems, and is used in furniture, plywood, veneers and interior joinery. It is sold in the U.S. as plywood under the copyrighted name Korina.

Mahogany, African, is shipped from west central Africa, and is a widely distributed and plentiful species, found in the coastal belt of the so-called high forest. *Khaya ivorensis* is the most favored and plentiful, while *K. antotheca* is found further inland. Heartwood is pale pink to a dark red-brown. The grain is often interlocked, and the texture is medium coarse, comparable to that of American mahogany. The wood seasons easily, but machining properties may vary. Nailing and gluing properties are good, and it takes an excellent finish. It also rotary peels easily for veneers, and is claimed to be moderately durable. Most uses are for furniture, boat work, cabinetry, interior finish and veneer.

Mahogany, American, also called Honduras mahogany, ranges from southern Mexico through Central America and into South America as far south as Bolivia. Plantations have been established throughout its natural range and elsewhere. Heartwood varies from a pale pink to a dark red-brown. Grain is generally straighter than that of African mahogany, but a wide variety of patterns may be found. Texture is fine to rather coarse. *Swietania macrophylla* air dries easily, without warping and checking difficulties. It rates as durable, and both heartwood and sapwood resist impregnation with preservatives. The wood works easily by hand and with power tools, and it slices into a rotary-cut veneer with no problems. It also takes a fine finish quite easily. Air-dry strength of mahogany is similar to American elm, and principal uses are for fine furniture and cabinetmaking, interior trim, pattern making, boat construction, fancy veneers, carving, and almost any other project where an attractive wood with exceptionally good dimensional stability is needed.

Mahogany, genuine. See "Gallery of Wood."

Mahogany, Philippine. See "Gallery of Wood."

Merbau comes from the Philippines, New Guinea and Malaya, and is also called ipil and kwila. *Intsia bijuga* is found throughout the Indo-Malay region, and into Australia, as well as on many of the western Pacific islands. Tree size is quite variable, but trunk diameter may be as much as 4 feet, and even a little more. Fresh-cut heartwood is a yellow color ranging to orange-brown, and turns brown to dark red-brown on exposure. Texture is fairly coarse, and the grain may be straight but is more apt to be wavy and interlocked. Quartersawn figures are striped with the interlocked grain, but otherwise the figure is plain. Air-dry strength is comparable to that of hickory, but the density is a little lower. Merbau seasons well, with little loss, but stains black in the presence of iron

and moisture. It gums saw-teeth and dulls cutting edges, so is difficult to work, but dresses smooth and takes a nice finish. It is not resilient, thus is inclined to brittleness. Merbau glues up well if mating faces are cleaned with alcohol. Durability and resistance to termite attack are good, and merbau is used in furniture, turnery, cabinetry, musical instruments and specialty items.

Obeche trees in west central Africa reach heights of 150 feet, with diameters to 5 feet. The trunk is usually free of branches for great heights, so clear lumber of good size is available. Wood is creamy white to pale yellow, with no clear difference between sapwood and heartwood. *Triplochiton scleroxylon* is a fairly soft wood with a uniform medium to coarse texture. The wood is relatively strong. It glues well, and takes stain well. The grain is sometimes straight, but more often interlocked, and the wood seasons readily with moderate to small losses from distortion and is resistant to decaying after drying. Quartersawing produces a stripe figure. Obeche works easily with hand and power tools, and takes nails and screws without problems with splitting. The wood is useful for veneers, boxes, millwork, pattern making and similar uses.

Padauk. See "Gallery of Wood."

Pau Marfim, sometimes called moroti, grows in a limited range from southern Brazil and Paraguay into northern Argentina. *Balfourodendron riedelianum* is a tree of middle size, up to about 85 or 90 feet, with a trunk about 30 inches thick. The heartwood is similar in appearance to the sapwood of maple,

though growth rings are not as distinctly present. The pale yellow color points up a fine, even texture, and the growth rings are visible in flat-sawn lumber. The grain is usually straight, but may on occasion be wavy. The wood is heavy, about on a par with hickory, and is strong and tough, more so than ash, but not as good as hickory. It dries fairly easily and takes a smooth finish. The wood is used for striking tool handles, should make good flooring, and the fine texture and light color suggest it as a substitute for boxwood for rules. It also turns well, and holds nails and screws strongly, though pilot holes are almost essential to easy working. It works readily with all sharp tools. The wood is not suitable for unprotected outdoor use.

Purpleheart. See "Gallery of Wood."

Ramin is one of a few moderately heavy woods that are classed as blond woods. *Gonystylus bancanus* is found throughout much of Southeast Asia, and was first introduced to the import market about 1950. The tree seldom has a trunk diameter over 2 feet, with a height of 80 feet being about tops, too. The heartwood and sapwood are both a pale, creamy color. Grain is usually straight, but may on occasion interlock. The wood is plain looking, with no wild or fancy figures in normal logs, but the texture is middling fine and even, much like true mahogany. Ramin is hard and heavy, but easy to work with all sharp tools, finishes nicely, and glues up with no extra preparation. Ramin is not durable, but accepts treatment, and also takes stains, paints and varnishes very well. The wood is used for furniture, veneer, toys and flooring.

Rosewood. See "Gallery of Wood."

Sapele occurs widely in tropical Africa and is a large rain forest tree, often 150 feet tall, with logs 40 inches and more in diameter. *Entandrophragma cylindricum* is a wood similar to mahogany in appearance, and has a notable striped figure when quartersawn. It sometimes has a fiddleback or mottled figure, and is darker in color, and finer in texture, than African mahogany. Sapwood may be 4 inches thick, and grain is interlocked, producing the narrow, uniform striped pattern mentioned. It has greater strength than white oak, and is a heavy wood that works easily with sharp tools, though, as often happens, the interlocked grain creates problems in planing and molding operations. Sapele takes finishes well and glues up nicely. The heartwood is moderately durable. It is used for decorative veneer, and is rotary-peeled for plywood; it is also used for window frames, staircases and flooring.

Satinwood comes from central and southern India and Sri Lanka, and is sometimes called East Indian satinwood. *Chloroxylon swietenia* is a small tree, no more than 50 feet in height, with a trunk diameter of about 1 foot. The wood is distinctive and good looking, ranging in color from a pale yellow to a golden yellow, with a fine, even texture. Grain is variable, sometimes wavy, sometimes interlocking, and produces decorative stripe or mottled figure when quartersawn. Gum veins may mar the looks. The wood is strong and durable, but fairly difficult to work and season. Satinwood tends to surface check and distort. It is hard on tools, dulling edges quickly, thus almost demanding carbide-cutting edges. It takes work, but satinwood can be brought to a truly fine finish. It turns nicely, but is hard to glue. Clean mating surfaces with alcohol, and make sure joints are tightly cut. Satinwood is used as an inlay and as a quarter-cut veneer, and solid wood is used for brush backs and small turned items.

Snakewood has a lot of names, including letterwood, leopard wood and tortoiseshell wood, indicating a range of patterns that may be found in the wood. *Piratinera guianensis* comes from a medium-sized tree, no more than 80 feet tall, and about 30 inches in diameter. Only the heartwood is of commercial interest because it is truly distinctive looking, with irregularly shaped dark markings somewhat like the markings on some snakes, or a little like Egyptian hieroglyphics (thus the name letterwood). The color is a deep mahogany red, with markings darker, almost black. Snakewood is strong but brittle, and almost twice as heavy as oak. The density makes snakewood a problem to season, and it tends to check and split while drying. It splinters readily, and splits along the grain, meaning screws must have pilot holes drilled and great care must be used during fastening. It is hard to cut, but takes a high natural finish, and is highly resistant to fungi. The wood is oily, like teak and cocobolo, so it is hard to glue. Use acetone, alcohol or lacquer thinner to swab off mating surfaces for best results. Snakewood is usually sold by weight, and may be difficult to locate. It is very expensive. It is used for umbrella handles, inlays and marquetry, and for bows for violins and other stringed instruments.

Teak. See "Gallery of Wood."

Tigerwood. See "Gallery of Wood."

Zebrawood. See "Gallery of Wood."

PART TWO

FELLING, MILLING AND DRYING WOOD

Chapter Five

FINDING AND FELLING WOOD

In this area, almost all woodworkers are novices, for not a great many of us take a chain saw into the woods to put the clip on a tree. The first problem is finding trees to cut if we desire to do that work ourselves.

FINDING WOOD

The process of finding trees to cut depends on local land ownership and your relationship to the local landowners. I'm assuming here that you don't have your own major acreage woodlot out of which you can log all you need and want. You may be able to buy trees for stumpage fees, which is the way most professional loggers get their basic material. But you may also be able to get so-called backyard trees for nothing, if you remove them. This can be an iffy proposition, and may involve buying special insurance and all sorts of special trimming needs. And it could even require lots of special equipment to prevent damage to homes and grounds. On farms, you'll probably have to pay a stumpage fee, but you can do the job with a simple chain saw and hard hat combination, added to the normal amount of care logging flat demands to prevent injury.

Felling trees is hard, dangerous work. Gain experience on smaller trunks, on flat ground, and then work up. Follow all safety manual instructions while felling trees!
Courtesy of Southern Forest Products Association.

Single trees brought to a mill can create problems, and you'd best talk them out with the mill operator first. The problems of transport, cutting schedule and removal are all solvable in normal ways, but if you're unable to assure the miller that you will replace damaged teeth on his blade, he may refuse to cut your log. Most will do the cutting if you assure them you're willing to make replacements, but be even more careful in tree selection if you do. Although a single tooth may cost only twelve to fifteen dollars, you should also be aware that a destroyed blade, should there be an old iron fence post embedded in the tree, can run a grand or even more. Fence-line trees are generally to be avoided for this reason, and also because they are bound to have at least several fence staples under the bark by the time they reach harvest size.

A detailed description of the process of felling a tree is beyond the scope of this book. The only information possible here is on how to drop the tree, assuming a fairly clear line of fall and some minor chain saw experience. You must select the tree and either bring in a portable sawmill—often the best and cheapest bet—or have the downed tree or trees hauled to a mill for cutting. We can tell you a bit about relative costs of band saw and chain saw mills, and give you some general operating instructions about cutting the wood yourself, but the differences in cost and work and overall practicality are great enough you must make the final comparison, and if necessary do the final learning of the operation yourself.

You'll find it is often possible to make a deal with the mill operator on costs. For example, the operator

Unloading logs is a first step at Mark Martin's sawmill.

may cut two trees in exchange for a third tree. Local trade-off rates vary, and you need to check around. First, find out the price of green wood of the species you want, cut and stacked at the mill. Then figure out how many board feet are in your logs, and see how much you're willing to trade for the mill operator to pick up (if possible) and saw the logs to order. Of course, you can also pay for the services if you've only got a single tree, or need all the lumber in your several trees. Again, that is negotiable, with much depending on the cut you require, the size of the logs, transport needs if any, time span required, and just how busy the mill is at the moment you need the work done. Most mills, like other businesses, drop prices in slack seasons and get back to normal, or above, in the busiest times.

Currently, and for some time past, a dime a board foot is about average for sawing logs in a straightforward manner. For specialized work, such as quartersawing, you may pay more. And, of course, if the mill also

has to pick up the logs (assuming the mill is even equipped to do so), that cost is added. Kiln drying also adds more than a dime a board foot to costs, and most small mills are not equipped to kiln dry; however, many can tell you the best place to get it done.

Assume, for example (and check these prices: They're used for examples and may vary widely from area to area and over time) that rough, green walnut is selling for about a dollar a board foot. If you have several trees that will produce 1,000 board feet of log-run walnut, then you need to make a deal for the work that's fair enough to both you and the mill. If you have three trees, though, you're not about to trade one for the cutting of the other two in a dime-a-board-foot sawing market! Or, say you have three oak logs grading out to almost the same size. You may have to pay with all of the third log, because if the lumber is less than 350 board feet, it is not worth more than 30 cents a foot green and rough.

Stacking logs to await debarking and milling is the second step.

Mark debarks trees as step #3.

EQUIPMENT AND YOUR PHYSICAL CONDITION

One thing is sure: If you're going logging, make sure you're in at least fairly good shape. Last August I got involved in a firewood-cutting deal with my local Marine Corps League chapter, thinking that though I was fat as a hog, I was in pretty good shape. Sure I was. Thirty minutes three times weekly on a stair climber,

and another hour lifting weights, doesn't do a thing for you, or at least not enough, when you're running a chain saw and lugging logs for hours in 99° heat. I had to pack it in before 3:30 P.M. and was probably lucky I didn't give myself a heart attack. As it was, I was, to put it mildly, off my feed and feeling absolutely awful for a couple of weeks, though my muscle tone was good enough—I had no

muscle soreness at all.

So watch it. Don't get overinvolved if you're not physically able to do the work. And don't kid yourself about logging being easy work. Neither it nor milling is anything like easy, and both are dangerous. So is felling trees. The chain saw is probably the single most dangerous tool available to the general public today, as it has been for decades. Even simple sawmills based on chain saws can be dangerous, though if handled correctly neither setup is that bad. Band saw sawmills aren't quite as dangerous, but are far more costly (the cheapest is about two and a half times the price of the fully equipped and set up Granberg chain saw mill).

You need at least two pairs of gloves for this kind of work. I can wear fairly heavy gloves with a chain saw and still work, and handling rough lumber works fine with similar gloves, but I'm at a loss when trying to use some of the canvas and leather gloves so many photos seem to feature. I lose too much feel for what I'm doing. Wells-Lamont produces their Grips series of gloves, and I've found the deerskin 970M (the M is for medium, so if you wear larger or smaller gloves, go for S or L or even XL) good for moderately heavy work; for winter I use lined 1030M gloves. For finer work, I wear either the super cheap gloves Leichtung sells, at about twenty dollars (including shipping) for three pairs, or Wells-Lamont's goatskin 1770M gloves. The goatskin gloves are the only ones I've ever found that allow me to handle even finer tools, though I still prefer to work bare-handed whenever possible.

Working bare-handed is not sensible, though, with chain saws, rough lumber, or for most actions with any

The Homelite 300 is a good medium-sized saw that will do everything except run the Granberg, or other, chain saw sawmills. It is too light for that work.

kind of sawmill. Nor is it sensible with lumber stacks, and when feeding lumber through planers. Sometimes it doesn't make sense when you're feeding jointers, either, and most especially if you're using the jointer in place of a planer.

Is finding and felling wood worth it, over time? That's something only you can say, but for a tool investment of less than $1,000, you can set up a chain saw mill and produce wood right where the tree drops, at a pace that provides a couple hundred board feet a day. Once the saw is amortized, you'll have only fuel, chains and wear and tear to figure into costs. But even with the cost of the mill and the huge chain saw to drive it (you need at least a 4-cubic-inch chain saw, and preferably one pushing 5 inches to drive the big Granberg mill), you will make out. If you do a lot of woodworking, finding and felling wood is worthwhile, as are other techniques in this book.

USING CHAIN SAWS

Safe chain saw use is something that we need to make sure of, but we also have to make sure of safe tree felling, limbing and bucking procedures at the same time. Use a chain saw safely and drop a tree on your head, and you have not done anything good. Use a chain saw safely and lop off a spring pole so it comes back and whacks your leg, smashing the bone, and you're missing a step. I've known people who have done both, and both guys believed they were using the saws safely because they carefully avoided saw kickback, and handled fuel properly.

Felling trees is difficult, hard work, and is inherently unsafe. Let's start with that premise and hold it solidly in mind.

Basic chain saw use starts with saw selection, and that relates largely to the size of the trees to be felled, limbed and bucked. For most purposes, the smallest saw size you'll want will be something with a 3-cubic-inch engine, and a 16-inch or 18-inch guide bar. If you're in an area with a lot of larger trees, and expect to be felling them, buy 4 or 5 cubic inches and go. Otherwise, rent a larger saw.

Safety starts with fueling. Gas and oil mixtures are not good for the forest floor, so use a funnel to help prevent spills. If the cans are full, place sheet plastic under the saw while filling. Keep your fueling station at least 25 feet from your cutting station, where you start the saw—don't walk around with a running chain saw.

When starting the saw, make sure the tool is well braced, and the chain is well away from your body or any other obstructions. Starting a saw with the tip almost resting on a limb is a good way to have it kick back as it starts, and kickback isn't smart. Keep bystanders out of the area. I do not know why this is so, but bystanders, including deer, seem to love chain sawing operations. You may have to ignore the deer, but keep people out of your way. The danger goes both ways, to you and them, so all bystanders must be well out of the line of fall in a 360-degree arc around the tree.

Under *no* circumstances, ever, try

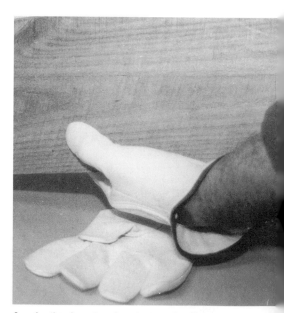

A reduction in cuts, abrasions and splinters makes goatskin gloves well worth their moderate cost.

to combine kids and chain saws. Children are often nearly impossible to keep track of, and you don't want to find one crushed under a felled tree. If children are around, there *must* be someone on hand to specifically care for them. Best of all is to make sure kids aren't there.

Your concentration needs to be on your own safety, and on the direction of the falling tree in relation to other trees, power lines, houses, other buildings and similar obstructions.

Bystanders must keep at least twice the estimated tree height from the cutting area.

Check your footing. Footing must be firm, and it's best to be able to operate the saw below chest level to keep proper control. Clear the footing area if needed, making sure wet, slick leaves and grass are removed. Get a proper grip on the saw during and after starting, with the left hand holding the bar and the thumb wrapped around the bar, and the right hand pulling straight up to start the saw. Keep a toe through the bottom part of the handle loop to keep the saw from moving.

Equipment will vary from person to person, but it's always a good idea to have a hard hat and safety glasses. Good work boots or shoes with cleated soles, such as the Vibram brand soles on so many work and hiking boots, are essential, and you may wish to wear gloves, and a pair of woodcutter's chaps with Kevlar fabric to stop chain saw cuts before they reach your legs. I can attest to the cutting power of even an idling chain, as many years ago I goofed and popped a knee with a chain saw. In an eye's blink, or less, the cut was down to the bone, and I was exceptionally unhappy on my way to the emergency room. That's with an idling chain!

Kickback

The more power the saw has, the bigger control problems it presents for occasional users. Kickback is more dangerous with added power, as the forces that induce it are stronger, as are normal push-pull forces. Kickback is the reaction of the saw that occurs when the nose section of the guide bar and the chain hit an object. Keep the nose of the saw from making accidental contact, and you have a good start at controlling kickback. Whenever you can, make your cuts well back on the straight parts of the bar. Use extra care when clearing whippy material such as underbrush. The sharper and better adjusted the chain, the lower the chances of kickback, too. If you've got to make a boring cut, using the bar and chain nose, use great care and make sure your grip is correct and very firm. Too, stand out of line of any possible kickback, with the saw to one side of your body, so that any kickback has to go over your shoulder instead of into your head or neck.

Pull is the action you get when you use the bottom of the bar to cut into the top of a log, with the saw's power pulling itself into the log.

The Poulan 3400, shown doing an underbuck on a log, is a good general-sized saw.

Keep the chain sharp and well adjusted. Adjustment on a sprocket nose chain means all the drive teeth are covered by the bar groove, and the chain just slips around the bar easily. Always wear gloves when adjusting and working on chains.

Courtesy of Poulan.

Push is the action you get when the top of the bar is used to cut into a log, when the saw's power pushes against you, forcing the saw back from the cut. As with kickback, push and pull are stronger with a more powerful saw.

A big part of the secret to safety in felling, limbing and bucking trees is balance. If you keep yours, then you stay out of trouble. To do this, you have to stay alert, including keeping an eye on the saw's progress. At the instant the cut is finished, the push or pull force stops, and you cut the throttle, thus allowing you to hold your balance, as you immediately stop reacting to the now nonexistent force.

Wear appropriate clothing, avoiding super-tight and super-sloppy clothes. Clothing that fits closely but not tightly is best and allows for fast movement. Leave all jewelry at home, whether a treasured pocket watch or a wedding ring or a necklace. A cheap wristwatch is OK, but don't wear a good one, as it is sure to attract a limb and get smashed.

Wear gloves. As I said earlier, I like the Grips series from Wells-Lamont. Chain saws vibrate like crazy and will raise a better than fair crop of blisters in a long day's cutting

if you don't protect your hands.

Eye protection cannot be overstated. If you wear glasses, make sure they have impact-resistant safety lenses, and consider buying some slip-on side shields for them. If you don't wear glasses, wear goggles or a face shield while cutting.

And the hard hat. Always wear a hard hat when working under trees where you cannot inspect the upper branches. It is a good idea, in fact, to always wear a hard hat when cutting any large tree, whether loose limbs are visible or not.

Wear earplugs or earmuff sound protectors. A chain saw is a noisy piece of machinery, and hearing loss from loud noises is cumulative.

From there, it's common sense ruling the day: Don't get overtired when working; don't work in drizzle or rain, snow or sleet (it gets too slick for escape if the tree goes the wrong way, and also gets slick enough to let you slip under trees, and into your own saw's chain); take a break when you get tired; don't use drugs or booze; avoid even prescription drugs unless you flat know they don't cause drowsiness; use leg muscles for heavy lifting and save your back; don't do heavy lifting, or other heavy work, without a careful check-up by your doctor before starting.

FELLING TREES

Felling, limbing and bucking aren't simple operations, regardless of how easy it seems to get a tree to fall and to saw it into lengths. The difficulty starts when you have to decide where the tree must go.

Once your tree is located, look up. Make sure there are no loose branches, "widowmakers," above you, and check for natural line of fall. If the tree has a slight lean, with most of the branches on the side leaned into, that's the way the tree wants to fall. It doesn't necessarily have to fall that way, but life is easier if it can be made to do so. Check for power lines, houses, decks, porches, patios, parked vehicles, roads, bystanders and other possible problems.

If the tree is a true sidehill plant (a really bad leaner), walk away from it. It will be reaction wood—tension or compression wood—and will be full of problems, even after it's down and seasoned.

Once a clear path of fall is determined, make sure you've got a clear path of retreat. Clear rocks and limbs out of the way, if necessary, and make the path at about a 45-degree angle to the line of fall. Tree butts often skip back towards the trunk when the tree falls, and it is far wiser

TREE FELLING TECHNIQUES

CAUTION
If the saw gets caught or hung up in a tree during felling, leave the saw and save yourself. The saw can be replaced and you cannot!

PLANNED LINE OF FALL

CLEAR PATH OF SAFE RETREAT 45° FROM LINE OF FALL

MAKE NOTCH AND BACKCUT TO FELL TREE IN DIRECTION PLANNED

PLANNED LINE OF FALL

AS TREE STARTS TO FALL, STOP THE ENGINE AND PUT SAW DOWN IMMEDIATELY

PLANNED LINE OF FALL

RETREAT ALONG CLEARED PATH, BUT WATCH THE ACTION IN CASE SOMETHING FALLS YOUR WAY

Clear and retreat.
Courtesy of Homelite.

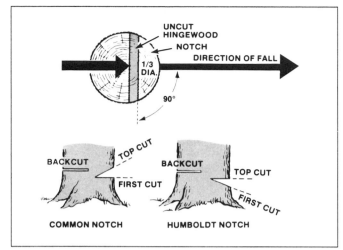

Notches.
Courtesy of Homelite.

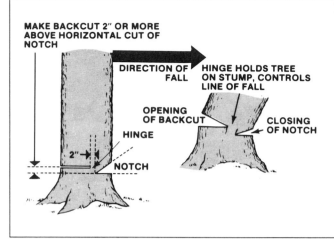

Backcut.
Courtesy of Homelite.

to be somewhere else when they pass through a space. The butt may or may not come back at you, but if it does, and the tree is a big one, the distance it kicks back can be startling.

Check the wind direction and force when felling. Along with the natural lean, wind direction has a lot to do with how easily a tree will fall on any particular point of the compass.

When you make your notch cut, check it for rotten wood. You're at a point where you've now got to bring the tree down, even if it's rotted, but use extra care when felling a rotted tree. That trunk will let go early, and may not follow a particular line of fall: Any tree may twist on its stump as it falls, but rotten ones twist sooner, and more, and more often, than do sound trees. Watch it, even if you know the tree is good only for firewood when it hits the ground. It can still drive you into the ground!

The first notch in felling trees is a directional tool (like a gun sight), and there are really two types. One, the common notch, has its first cut made parallel to the ground. The Humboldt notch is what you'll more likely use here, and it has the top, or

second, cut parallel to the ground. This gives a flat-ended log butt.

Make the back cut about 2 inches above the parallel cut, or, for large trees, go up the tree about 10 percent of the estimated log diameter (3 inches for a 30-inch-diameter trunk, and so on, but never less than 2 inches). Make that back cut as level as you can, for uneven back cuts tend to give you barber chair stumps, with a central patch of wood sticking up where the tree twisted and split off the stump, wasting much of the log. And don't cut all the way through to the notch, ever! That hinge of wood helps both in controlling the fall of the tree and preventing kickback of the butt. If necessary, use soft aluminum or plastic wedges to fell the tree the rest of the way—do not use steel splitting wedges, in case you have to come in and cut some more.

If the saw hangs up while the tree is starting to go, leave it and get the blazes out of there. Even with the best insurance in the world, replacing the most costly chain saw is cheaper than a mass of injuries. This is a basic tenet of chain saw use in the woods: If in doubt, drop the saw and clear out. The saw is easily replace-

able. Use wedges early when felling large trees, so that settling back of the trunk is prevented.

Limbing

Once the tree is down, limbing is the next primary chore, after which the tree is cut into transportable logs for travel to the mill. If you're using a portable sawmill, you may not be transporting trees, but later will cart the boards home.

Again, an examination of the area is needed. Some limbs will be under stress and may fly out and hit you if care isn't used in cutting them loose. For that reason, always work from the side opposite the one on which you're cutting off limbs. Reach over the tree to make the cuts, in other words. Don't climb on a tree to cut limbs if you can avoid doing so. And don't cut off every limb; leave a few to support the trunk so bucking is made easier. Trim the last branches after the trunk is bucked into logs.

Bucking

Bucking is simply the process of cutting a tree into logs. You either overbuck or underbuck. Overbucking is cutting from the top of the log

Cutting the felling notch.
Courtesy of Poulan.

Making the felling cut — note the distance above the lower, flat cut of the falling notch. At least 2 inches is essential here.
Courtesy of Poulan.

Whenever possible, limb on side opposite that where you're standing.
Courtesy of Poulan.

down, while underbucking reverses that and is cutting up from the underside of the log. Examining the trunk will give an idea of how the stresses are going to work, which helps to determine which type of bucking you use. If the tree appears apt to settle down in a way that will pinch the bar in an overbuck, use an underbuck. Start with the overbuck, going about a third of the way into the log, and finish up with an underbuck. If the log seems to have set up so it will rise as the cut is finished,

start with an underbuck and finish with an overbuck through the final two-thirds of the log.

When bucking a log, *always* stand on the uphill side if there is one. Under no circumstances, even on a slight grade, should you stand downhill of a log being bucked.

Logs are cut into sensible, usable lengths. If you never use boards over 6 feet long, then don't cut saw logs that are 8 feet and longer. If you have to have boards that are at least 10 feet long, then don't cut all saw logs

8 feet long. You should give some thought to your real needs. It's nice to be able to say you've got a real mess of lumber in 10-foot lengths, but when was the last time you did any woodworking with lumber over 6 feet long? I sure don't do any, and most of my woodworking friends are quite happy with 4-foot-long lumber, with the occasional piece 6 or 8 feet long.

At this point in time, you've got your saw logs ready to either transport or mill.

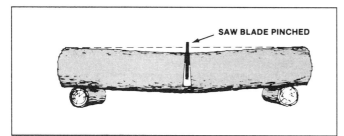

How a saw gets pinched.
Courtesy of Homelite.

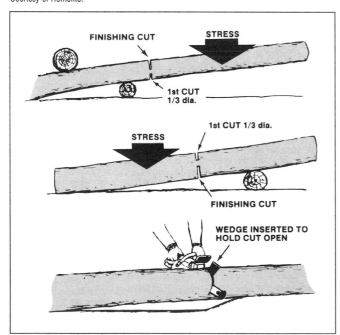

Proper bucking techniques.
Courtesy of Homelite.

A peavy, or log cant, is nearly essential to handling logs during bucking and milling operations.

Chapter Six

MILLING YOUR OWN WOOD

Sawing around the board produces the most lumber from a log.

The most common method of milling a tree is to saw around the board. The board thus produced has flat grain. Flat-sawn lumber is not best for some types of woodworking projects because it mixes sapwood and heartwood; the different densities of the sapwood and heartwood may make the board warp and cup. Flat-sawn lumber is identified by U- or V-shaped grain patterns at board ends. It's often all that's available, so it must be used. Make sure flat-sawn wood is as stable (dry) as possible.

Quartersawn lumber is more expensive than flat sawn, and is cut at a 90-degree angle to the growth rings. It mixes less heartwood and sapwood in each board, so it cups and warps less. Quartersawn logs are first cut in half, then each half is cut in half, giving four sections, or quarters. Quarters are cut from the outside in, with the radial section mak-

Later passes show the results of flat sawing.

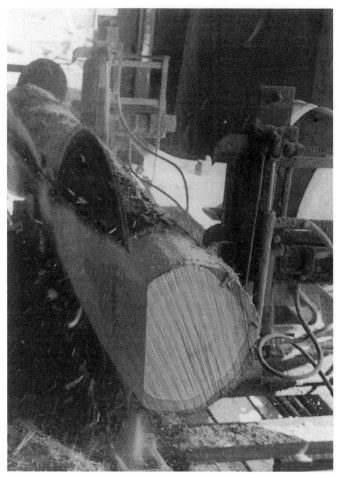

Mark Martin's sawmill is about two miles up the road from my house: Here, Mark is running a flat-sawing operation to produce oak construction timbers.

ing parallel grain lines.

Rotary cutting, or peeling, of logs produces veneers and plywoods: More costly veneers use half-round slicing, or quarter slicing (using a knife to take very thin — often as little as ¹⁄₂₈-inch-thick — slices). Slicing produces little waste.

Milling is covered more extensively later on, when we examine the use of home sawmills (band saw and chain saw sawmills) to produce lumber from logs.

Once the tree is down, you see the cross section of the trunk and note some clearly defined features of the wood. Bark is the outer part, and it is of variable thickness depending on the type and age of the tree: The

inner part of the bark is alive and usually thinner than the outer layer, which is cork-like and dead. Next is the wood, which is usually readily visible as sapwood and heartwood. In the center you find the pith, a small central core, often darker in color, which is the primary growth formed when the wood stems or branches get longer.

Often, the commercial logger has an end use for the tree in mind before cutting is begun: In most cases, the logger knows what the resulting wood will be used for — or, at least, that it will be *wood*, and not wood pulp, that will be used. Such knowledge is essential, for pulpwood trees are much smaller than lumber trees,

and it's only in the past year or two that pulp mills (paper producers) have decided they're just as happy receiving mixed hardwoods as they are taking in softwoods such as yellow pine. Few pulp mills want trees more than 8 inches in diameter, though they'll take a few larger ones per load (within a small range, say to 12 inches).

Knowing the final use means checking the tree to make sure it will make lumber — obviously, rotted, undersized, gnarled and twisted trees are not much good for commercial lumber operations, and often end up as firewood. Some of those gnarled trees, some runt trees and even a few slightly rotted trees may very well make lumber for us, though.

Gnarled trees tend to have lots of burl and otherwise fancy-figured wood, and while some tree species seldom get much over the runt stage (for our purposes, let's classify runt trees as anything under 25 feet in height and 12 inches in diameter), they provide some beautifully figured, durable and generally lovely wood. Apple trees serve as superb examples of both types. Seldom do they get over 25 feet tall, and if they get over a foot in diameter, the tree is probably a century old and partly rotted inside. But the figure and grain is superb in many of these trees, and they're well worth the effort of the home lumbermaker.

Making one's own lumber is a different procedure than producing lumber for sale. We're not looking to make a profit, except by virtue of time spent enjoyably, and in expenses reduced for later projects. Lumbermaking is a project, or series of projects, that requires extreme patience—the number of times I've been tempted to use half-dry lumber mounts almost daily, but I usually avoid the lure because the results are so poor. But it also allows a lot of leeway in wood selection, leeway you may not find, and in fact, almost certainly will not find, in a local lumberyard.

Some specialist mills, such as Groff & Hearne of Quarryville, Pennsylvania (800-342-0001 for their latest price list, and tell 'em I told you to call) sell lumber that otherwise is outrageous in price at rational prices, and in a far wider variety than is often available locally. Of course, prices are usually FOB whatever the location of the sawmill, so that's added cost, but there are no other stable sources of things such as sassafras (a low-cost wood), flame birch (moderate cost), tiger maple (low to moderate cost), paulownia, pumpkin pine, curly cherry (moderate to high cost), and butternut in 4/4 FAS and other grades. (We'll take a look at hardwood grades shortly.) Groff & Hearne also carries 4/4 apple, aromatic cedar to 6/4 size, locust, pearwood, Kentucky coffee wood in 4/4 and 8/4, basswood in 8/4 and 16/4, longleaf yellow pine up

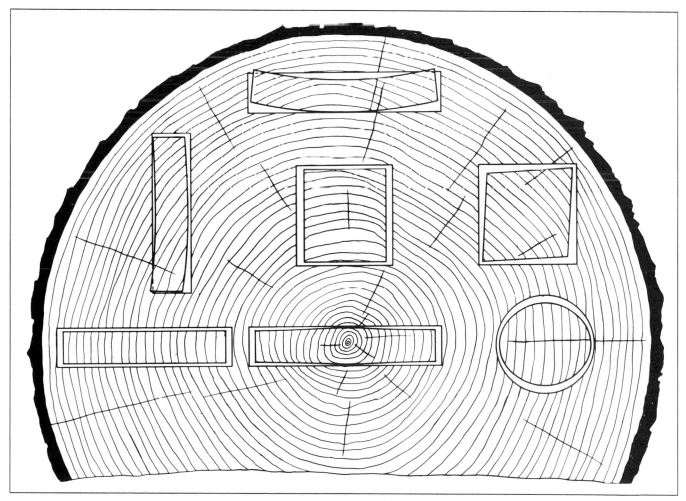

Characteristic shrinkage and distortion of wood. Tangential shrinkage is double radial shrinkage.

Your boards won't come off your home mill this prolifically, but, then, you won't need the space and equipment.
Courtesy of Georgia-Pacific Corporation.

to 12/4 and persimmon in 4/4.

Groff & Hearne's real bragging point is that they carry lumber, including cherry, walnut, white oak, maple and butternut, in widths to 40 inches. Most of their boards are available in widths 10 inches and greater for a slight premium per board foot.

Other places, such as Woodcraft and The Woodworkers' Store, carry domestic and exotic lumbers in a moderate range of sizes, surfaced four sides (S4S is the way that's usually designated) at higher cost. The Woodworkers' Store also has a moderately wide line of domestic and exotic furniture-quality plywood panels, in sizes that UPS will deliver without extra charges.

I'm not going to get involved here with modulus of elasticity, modulus of rupturability, elastic properties, Poisson's ratios (all six!) and the other arcane measures of strength and utility for woods, for a variety of reasons. Foremost among those reasons is the fact that it is only in the very odd case that any woodworker needs to know the difference in the modulus of elasticity of, for example, green and dry jack and loblolly pines. Also, I've already covered the essential properties in the descriptions of the woods themselves. In addition I included other features that may help woodworkers determine if a particular wood is worth bothering with for a specific project: One is how hard it is to work, includ-

ing machining, nailing, screwing and general handling; another is how easily it glues up with normal woodworking adhesives.

HOME SAWMILLS

There are two primary types of home sawmills. Two versions mount on chain saws and cost very little extra money, while a band saw version fits on wheels and costs a small fortune (there are cheaper versions of the band saw mill, too, but none I know of go for under $3,000, and a number of the top models are over $10,000).

With either type of these mills, the length of the saw log isn't important, except as it affects cutting time. I'm going to describe the general operation of the Granberg chain saw-mill, because the operation is fairly simple and basic, while the operation of the Wood-Mizer LT25 is a whole other story. That's one you may want to find locally and rent, along with an operator, for a day or two of wood cutting, where its 1000-board-foot-per-day capacity can be put to great use. It is much too complex and costly for the average wood-worker—or even the way above average, I'm afraid. The machine is delightful, lives up to expectations, and works well, but takes practice to operate properly, and costs a solid penny.

The Granberg Alaskan MK III, in contrast, is far less speedy, offers far fewer types of milling (I've never even heard of anyone quartersawing with one of these, and sawing round the log and quartersawing are both easy options for the Wood-Mizer), and chomps out a nearly ⅜-inch-wide kerf (compared to under 1/16

inch for the Wood-Mizer), so it wastes much more material.

But the MK III is low cost, though you do need a sizable saw to operate it, one that will drive a 36-inch-long bar to get the final 30-inch-long cut capacity. Mill, saw and everything you need shouldn't run a whole lot over $650 or $700 (dual power head units are available to work faster). The mill itself mounts quickly on the saw, and dismounts about as quickly, with no need to drill holes in the bar.

A guide rail, or plank, is placed on the log, and the top is slabbed off. The process is repeated on two more sizes, after which lumber is milled to the exact size you desire. Set the thickness on the vertical thickness rails on the mill, and start cutting: In most cases, you will want to cut boards intended for ¾-inch thickness to a thickness of 1⅛ inches. This allows for losses to drying and to planing.

For those really intending to get into this setup, I'd suggest buying at least two of the correct size of ripping chain, slabbing rail brackets (a lot easier to use than a plank, and more precise), a helper handle, one double-end saw bar in 44-inch length (for those with a huge saw and big trees, the double-end bars come in widths to 66 inches) and an oiler kit. You can then produce lumber from ½ inch to a full foot thick.

The larger and more powerful the saw, the quicker the unit works.

The descriptions don't provide much detail, I'm afraid, but to do any more on either wouldn't serve: The Wood-Mizer is beyond the capabilities of almost all woodworkers; the Granberg mill is simple enough to be rapidly learned, without any more help from me.

The uses of both are great, but the Wood-Mizer is the kind of tool you need to find locally. That is, you need to find some local person run-

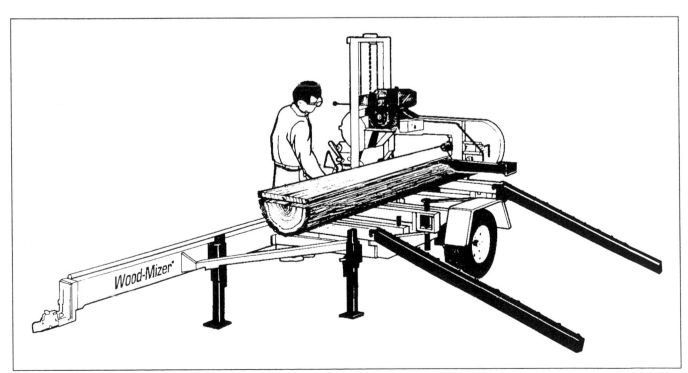

Wood-Mizer LT 25 in use.
Courtesy of Wood-Mizer.

ning one, full- or part-time, and talk him or her into coming into the woods with you to reduce your felled trees to lumber. The cost should be reasonable. In a very few areas, you may find one for rent, though it seems unlikely to me, because the very nature and complexity of the machinery makes it difficult to rent.

There is a third choice, the Haddon chain sawmill. It is smaller and even less complex than the Granberg, but is much slower to use. Still, the Granberg mills mounted on a 3.5-cubic-inch saw are slow, as is the Haddon: The Granberg can be readily attached to any existing chain saw with an engine of at least 3.5 cubic inches. That will give you the capacity to reduce the occasional tree to lumber, at a cost that probably won't exceed $250. You can add accessories—double-ended bar, helper handle, oiler, larger chain saw—as you see a need.

On a real basis, however, the Alaskan MK III is a good buy for woodworkers aiming to save a few bucks by making their own lumber.

GRADING SOFTWOODS AND HARDWOODS

Softwoods generally fall under structural lumber grading methods, and are divided into three primary categories: appearance lumber, stress-graded lumber and non-stress-graded lumber.

Appearance softwood grades are the highest, as they are in hardwoods, and are normally listed as Select or Finish. You find select and finish interior grades marked B and Better *(B&BTR)*: This is the highest grade generally available today. Appearance grades, no matter how pretty, are not necessarily the strongest, because there are no limits on

such faults as grain deviations, density, growth rings per inch and others. For structural lumber, stress-graded materials are needed.

Stress-graded materials, such as structural 2×4s, are graded Construction, Standard and Utility. Structural planking (2×6s, 2×8s, etc.) is graded as Select Structural No. 1, No. 2 and No. 3. Such lumber is grade-stamped at the mill, unless you are dealing with small local mills that provide you with air-dried or green unplaned lumber. The use of such lumber, in recent years, has been severely limited for residential structures. If you have any intention of using it outside of woodworking purposes, check building codes before you start, or you may face tearing down all or part of a structure.

Most softwood will be stamped KD if kiln-dried.

Hardwood lumber is sawed largely as factory lumber. Supplied in random widths and lengths (though your local supplier will usually provide widths and lengths to suit), factory lumber comes in a number of grades.

The grades are Firsts, Seconds, Firsts and Seconds or FAS, Selects, and then Common, starting with No. 1 and dropping to 3B. For our purposes, anything under a No. 2 Common (minimum clear width, one face, 3 inches by 2 feet) is useless.

Most hardwood sold today is FAS. You get clear lengths at least 3 inches by 7 feet, or 4 inches by 5 feet, with over 81 percent of the face clear of defects, on a board width of 6 inches and a length of from 8 feet to 16 feet. Dropping down to Selects gives 83 percent clear of defects, but on a board width of 4 inches and lengths from 6 feet to 16 feet. Clear cutting requirements are the same.

It normally does not pay to shop for lumber lower than Select grade, though for small projects, if you can pick and choose, the top two common grades, No. 1 and No. 2, may provide somewhat cheaper possibilities. For larger hardwood projects, FAS is almost imperative.

You will have to join several narrow boards edge to edge to create wide boards for projects that require them, unless you are both lucky and rich. Edge-joined wide boards tend to be more stable than single-piece wide boards anyway, and can be matched for figure to appear one piece.

DEFECTS IN WOOD

Examining lumber for purchase, you will note some defects that are obvious. But some may not become obvious until later, as you may find internal pin knots that don't appear on the surfaces. At this point, some knowledge of major visible defects can help you save money on wood.

Wane is bark along the edge of the board, or missing wood along the edge of the board, usually caused by bark dropping off.

Checking is the splitting of the board, usually at the ends, but sometimes at other spots.

Cupping is warping across the width of a board.

Warping is any distortion of the shape of the wood.

Crook is a form of warping, a deviation from end-to-end straightness.

Crack is a large radial check.

Diamonding is a form of warp, when a section of a board twists clockwise or counterclockwise, and thus appears as a diamond.

Sap stain is a bluish stain caused by fungi in and on the surface of the wood.

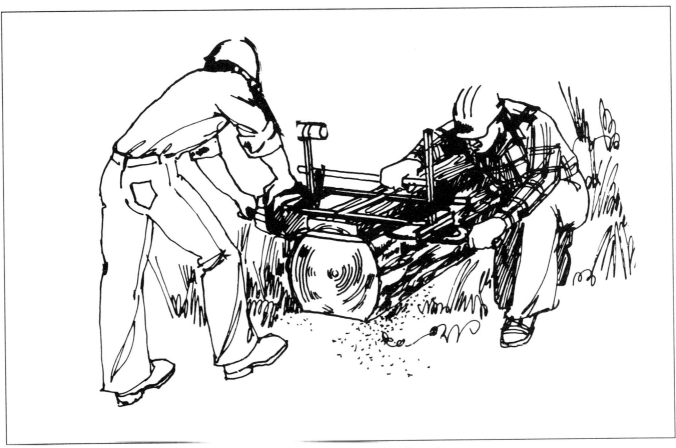

Granberg Alaskan MK III. This double-end sawmill may be used with an extra handle, and a second power head may be added for greater speed.

Courtesy of Granberg.

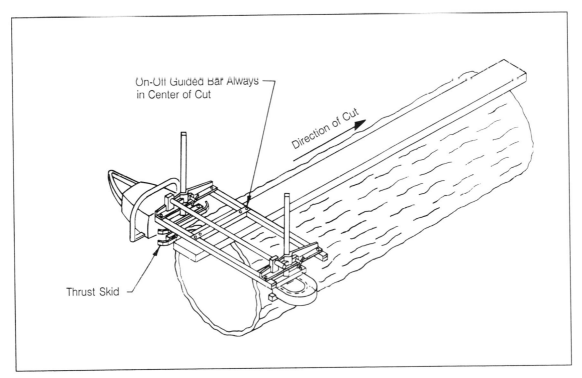

Granberg sawmill.

Courtesy of Granberg.

Knots are parts of branches that the expanding tree has overgrown.

1. *Pin knots* are less than a quarter-inch in diameter, while a spike knot has been cut along its long axis, giving its exposed section a stretched appearance.
2. *Encased*, or *black*, *knots* are knots that are loose but remain in the tree, trapped by later growth.
3. *Solid knots* are solid throughout the board and show no signs of rot or looseness.

WOOD DENSITY

Wood density is weight per cubic foot, or the ratio of the volume of the wood to the volume of water displaced. Because wood expands and contracts in taking on and losing internal water, density is an ever-changing measurement, but on a relative basis remains reasonably constant from wood species to wood species.

Density is measured with wood dried to a specific water content. Because wood movement affects stability of projects, and wood movement is affected by moisture content, wood density ratings are important, and must be done so that we can tell how the wood will react at the time we are working on it, and later. We can honestly say density measurements are fairly rough, but they give us a useful amount of information about a particular wood or group of woods. Density is a way to determine ease of working a species of wood:

Denser woods are harder to machine. Hardness almost directly relates to density—the denser any wood, the harder it is. Denser woods are harder to fasten, but they hold fasteners much better than less dense woods.

Specific gravity (the method we use to rate density) of our most common softwoods runs from 0.28 to 0.59. Domestic hardwoods range from 0.35 (cottonwood, basswood and butternut) to 0.88 (pignut hickory, our hardest commonly available wood). Imports go from balsa's very light 0.15 up to lignum vitae's 1.23; lignum vitae doesn't float, while balsa was once the material used to make life rafts for ships where floating was its reason for being.

TABLE OF DENSITIES

North American Softwood Densities

Wood Specific Gravity, Dry		Fir, noble	0.39	Pine, red	0.46
Bald cypress	0.46	Fir, Pacific silver	0.43	Pine, sand	0.48
Cedar, Alaska	0.44	Fir, subalpine	0.32	Pine, shortleaf	0.51
Cedar, Atlantic white	0.32	Fir, white	0.39	Pine, slash	0.59
Cedar, Eastern red	0.47	Hemlock, Eastern	0.40	Pine, spruce	0.44
Cedar, incense	0.29	Hemlock, mountain	0.45	Pine, sugar	0.36
Cedar, Northern white	0.31	Hemlock, Western	0.45	Pine, Virginia	0.48
Cedar, Western red	0.32	Larch, Western	0.52	Pine, Western white	0.38
Douglas fir, Coast	0.48	Pine, Eastern white	0.35	Redwood, old-growth	0.40
Douglas fir, Interior north	0.48	Pine, jack	0.43	Redwood, young-growth	0.35
Douglas fir, Interior south	0.46	Pine, loblolly	0.51	Spruce, black	0.42
Douglas fir, Interior west	0.50	Pine, longleaf	0.59	Spruce, Engelmann	0.35
Fir, balsam	0.35	Pine, pitch	0.52	Spruce, red	0.40
Fir, California red	0.38	Pine, pond	0.56	Spruce, Sitka	0.40
Fir, grand	0.37	Pine, ponderosa	0.40	Spruce, white	0.36

North American Hardwood Densities

Wood Density		Elm, slippery	0.53	laurel	0.63
Alder, red	0.41	Hackberry	0.53	northern red	0.63
Ash, black	0.49	Hickory, pecan:		pin	0.60
Ash, blue	0.58	Bitternut	0.66	scarlet	0.67
Ash, green	0.56	Nutmeg	0.60	water	0.63
Ash, white	0.60	Pecan	0.66	willow	0.69
Aspen, bigtooth	0.39	Hickory, true:		Oak, white:	
Aspen, quaking	0.38	Mockernut	0.72	burr	0.64
Basswood	0.37	Pignut	0.75	chestnut	0.66
Beech	0.64	Shagbark	0.72	live	0.88
Birch, paper	0.55	Shellbark	0.69	overcup	0.63
Birch, sweet	0.65	Locust, black	0.69	post	0.67
Birch, yellow	0.62	Magnolia, cucumber tree	0.48	swamp chestnut	0.67
Butternut	0.38	Magnolia, Southern	0.50	swamp white	0.72
Cherry, black	0.50	Maple, bigleaf	0.48	white	0.68
Chestnut	0.43	Maple, black	0.57	Sassafras	0.46
Cottonwood, balsam poplar	0.34	Maple, red	0.54	Sweetgum	0.52
		Maple, silver	0.47	Sycamore, American	0.49
Cottonwood, black	0.35	Maple, sugar	0.63	Tupelo, black and water	0.50
Cottonwood, Eastern	0.40	Oak, red:		Walnut, black	0.55
Elm, American	0.50	black	0.61	Willow, black	0.39
Elm, rock	0.63	cherrybark	0.68	Yellow poplar	0.42

Chapter Seven

DRYING WOOD

The process of getting rough lumber ready to use for a cabinet or toy varies considerably at home from what you will see in a commercial operation. But the result must be about the same: a good piece of wood, dried to 8 to 10 percent moisture content (down to 6 to 8 percent for your super-critical needs), with enough clear cutting to suit the project in hand.

To begin, you must find the required space and then get together the necessary materials. If you're going to just air dry wood down to about 15 percent moisture content, and then farm it out for the remainder of the drying, you've simplified things considerably.

Stickered wood moves into the drying kiln.
Courtesy of Georgia-Pacific Corporation.

SPACE REQUIREMENTS

For air drying, you need space, preferably out in the sun, if you don't have a shed for drying. Shade is okay if you're not close enough to a tree to have problems with wet leaves, bird droppings, small limbs and other debris. But an open, sunny space is better, as it allows faster and more trouble-free air drying.

Make sure the space over which you stack wood is dry. Boggy conditions do not aid drying. And try to face one end of any stack into the

prevailing wind for your area. Here that's west-northwest.

The amount of space needed, of course, depends on the size and number of stacks. I'd suggest using 8-foot-long lumber most of the time. Also, it's said to serve best if you stack wood for air drying in the same order in which it was cut from the tree. That can make for some strange-looking stacks, if you can even remember the order you sliced wood from the tree; if another sawyer did the job, forget it. Just get the

wood stacked as close to level as possible, and properly stickered, and then cover the top. Stickers are pieces of dried, straight wood about 1 inch by 1 inch square (may be as small as 3/4 inches square, but no thinner), and of appropriate length to fit across the stack. Stickers are placed about every 24 to 30 inches along the length of the stack, at 90-degree angles to the stacked boards. Each row of drying boards is stickered before another row is laid. A 4-foot by 8-foot stack is easily covered

Dried, rough soft maple stored at Sam Moore's Furniture Company.

with a couple of sheets of galvanized roofing, or a single sheet of plywood.

MOISTURE METERS

Air dry the wood for a year for each inch of thickness, if air drying is all it's going to get. Keep a check on moisture content with a meter. I have a couple of good meters, a little Lignomat and a slightly more costly Delmhorst, both of which do a fine job of letting me know what's what internally with the wood. There is a new meter I've yet to try; it works without penetrating the wood, supposedly creating fewer problems with finished woods.

You do need a moisture meter to properly season wood. Prices range from about thirty-five dollars, delivered, on up to about what you're willing to pay, but most of the accurate and durable Lignomat and Delmhorst meters cost from three to five times that thirty-five-dollar figure. You need a meter with a bottom range that includes 6 percent, but the top range need not go beyond 20 percent.

MATERIALS

In addition to a moisture meter, you need gloves, stickers, some cement blocks, a few pressure-treated land-scape timbers, a sheet or two of heavy black plastic, and as many pieces of metal or plastic roofing as it takes to cover the top of the wood. You may also use Exterior grade ply-wood to cover the top of the wood. Anything else, such as board end sealer, is gravy. Woodcraft's SealTite 60 can help reduce cracking and checking of board ends. Constantine's also offers the product, as does The Woodworkers' Store and a number of others, including local specialty lumber dealers.

STACKING LUMBER

To get the timbers well off the ground, lay out the cement blocks over the plastic sheet in a pattern that supports each timber at 3-foot inter-vals or less. The plastic prevents ground moisture from passing up into the stack and extending the dry-ing time. Make sure the timbers are laid out to support your lumber sizes.

Start by stacking boards directly on the timbers, crossways. Make a row that way, and sticker as you go, plac-ing 1-inch by 1-inch stickers at 2-foot or closer intervals to support the next row. Keep board edges about 1 inch apart so there's room for air flow. Don't build the stack so high it totters or the first wind will blow it over.

Sticker material must be clean and dry. Do not ever use wet sticker material, whether because the sticker wood is green, or stickers have been in the weather. Wet stickers create stains running crossways in the boards. It is also best if stickers are made of the same wood as that being dried, though it's far from always possible. If, for example, and as hap-pened to me recently, you're drying your first load of walnut, you may have to use oak or (preferably) pop-

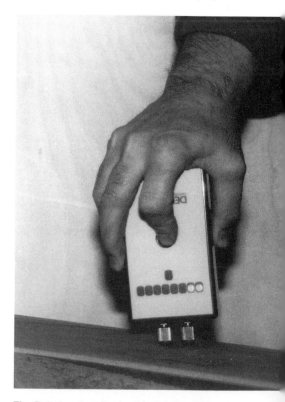

The Delmhorst meter is showing 8 percent moisture content in a piece of red oak. That means the wood is ready for any use, includ-ing cabinetmaking.

lar as the sticker material.

Before fooling with stickers, though, select your lumber. Results are going to be better if you remember the old computer user's adage: GIGO. Garbage in, garbage out. The better the wood you start drying, the more, and better, wood you'll finish drying.

Select the straightest-grained wood you can find, with as few knots, sap pockets and other defects as possible. Highly figured wood, no matter the wood or the pattern, always checks more than straight-grained wood. Naturally, if you want to use highly figured wood, you plan for greater losses.

Use stock from 1 inch to 2 inches thick. Actually sawmill thickness should be 1⅛ inches or 2⅛ inches to allow for planing and drying losses. Of course, you may have wood milled, or mill it yourself, as thin as you like, but try to hold a minimum of ½ inch for a final ⅜-inch lumber, or ⅜ inch for final ¼-inch lumber. Most planers won't handle anything thicker, and thin stuff may cup and warp more. Also, thicker boards don't dry evenly, and take much longer to dry.

Try to avoid using wood with ends already checked. End grain loses water in a rush, about ten times as fast as the rest of the wood, so checks are going to happen. Cutting off checks and coating fresh end grain with sealer helps stop checking. If you don't wish to use a commercial sealer, such as SealTite 60, try using asphalt roofing compound or fibrated aluminum roofing compound. Those are much cheaper and almost as effective, but are messier to apply and will gum a saw blade if you do a sloppy application job and get it down to the bit you need to cut off

after drying. Whatever you do, add a total of 6 inches to board lengths for final trim needs.

Dry boards that are narrower than a foot. The wider the boards you dry, the more cupping and warping you'll experience. Wood shrinkage across the width is far greater than lengthwise shrinkage, so wide boards create problems.

When wood is stacked, add a row of rougher boards at the top, and then cover the entire stack with a sheet of plywood or roofing, and weight the cover down with cement blocks. If sunshine is exceptionally strong in an area, cover the sides with canvas to retard moisture loss.

Caring for the Stack

There's not a lot to do once a proper stack is made. Keep debris, including grass, from building up around and on the stack, and keep an eye out for boards that warp and knock the stack out of shape. Remove such boards and restack neatly. Also, keep an eye on the drying rate. If the boards are drying too fast, you'll find too much checking and warping and will have to add protection from the sun. If boards are drying too slowly, you'll see stains from mold, and possibly even mushrooms growing. Take off any side covers and, if necessary, restack to open the pile up to the sun and wind. You may have to restack to allow as much as 3 inches between boards as they're relaid nice and flat.

Drying Time

The old rule of thumb stated that you leave wood to be air dried a full year for each inch of thickness, and that still works well with wood over 2 inches thick. For wood in the ½- to 2-inch range, where we're mostly

going to be, you will want to use a moisture meter, because in the hot seasons of the year, you may find that wood approaching 15 percent humidity levels within forty-five days. We're assuming here that your weather is not like mine, where summers are hot and humid. Temperate days with lots of sun are best, of course, but we can't order those up like breakfast. Humidity levels need to be reasonable, so throughout the South in summer, add at least thirty days to the forty-five-day time.

To get below 15 percent moisture levels, you need to reduce the humidity around the wood, and you cannot do this outdoors. For final results, move the wood indoors to an area that approximates the humidity you wish to attain, and in a few weeks the wood will match the new, lower humidity. Different woods take differing times to reach air-dry equilibrium. Basswood is about the fastest hardwood to dry, while white oak is going to take almost 50 percent longer. Or you may choose to finish the wood off in either your own solar kiln or a commercial kiln.

Once the wood is finished, with a measured moisture content of 10 percent or less, it needs to be protected from exposure to wind and rain: It must be stored indoors to retain its low moisture content. At this point, you remove the stickers and stack the wood in a solid block. (If you can get hold of banding equipment for wood to be stored more than a week or so, it can help wood hold its shape, but for us, it isn't worth buying the equipment needed.) The solid block helps prevent excess wood movement and transmission of humidity through the stack. Do not cut the sealed ends off until just before you begin to joint and plane the wood.

If wood is not to be used immediately, leave it unfinished and stickered in outdoor stacks.

SOLAR DRYERS

Solar dryers can reduce drying time considerably, and there need be nothing fancy about their construction. A basic 6-foot-wide, 6- to 8-foot-tall and 8-foot-long building provides room for about 700 to 800 square feet of wood, and will take it from green to cabinet-dry (8 percent) in about two months. You'll need to restack at that time, for the dried wood will only be the top quarter or third, while the bottom of the stack may retain as much as 50 percent more water (about 12 percent). Obviously your stacking style, orientation of the building, and area of the country all have an effect on the drying rate. You'll need to experiment

and test with some constancy to make sure your wood is where you want it to be, but this solar dryer provides the finishing touches for almost any wood in fairly short order—and it works much faster with wood that is thoroughly air dried.

The shed may be built for under five hundred dollars in almost every area of the country, and locally available materials may make a considerable difference in the construction cost. I've listed, for example, Warp Brothers Flex-O-Pane, but you may find a local source of heavy plastic sheeting, or even acrylic storm door sheet, for low or no cost (but don't bet on it). You also may find old glass doors available from time to time. When considering such uses, check with contractors who build decks and install replacement windows—they also do doors; patio doors work best. The Flex-O-Pane is listed be-

cause it's the clearest heavy, flexible sheet plastic I have found, and transmission of heat is assisted by the clearness. Flex-O-Glass is a 4-mil version of the 10-mil Flex-O-Pane, and is more suitable for super cold applications, where temperatures are apt to be well below zero for several days at a time.

To build the dryer, start with post holes or with foundations. I'm using foundations, taking one small bag of Quikrete or Sakrete each, because I have on hand 4 × 6 and 4 × 4 and 6 × 6 pressure-treated lumber from earlier projects, which is too short to set into holes. It's cheaper to use that than to buy anything new, because the unit (mine will be 16 feet long) only requires six major vertical members. My floor is to be gravel over three layers of heavy sheet plastic (10 mil). Intermediate framing is 2 × 4, rough cut (straight from the sawmill,

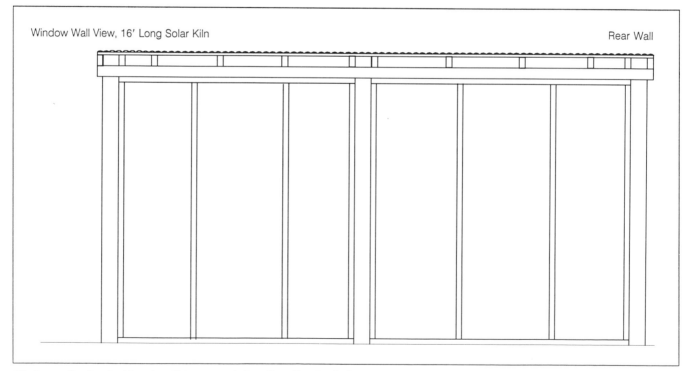

Window wall solar shed framing. Note corrugated roofing: Use the darkest color roofing you can locate to help build heat in the solar shed. The window wall of any solar drying kiln should be located so the rising sun shines in. Face this wall east, or southeast to east-southwest for best results.

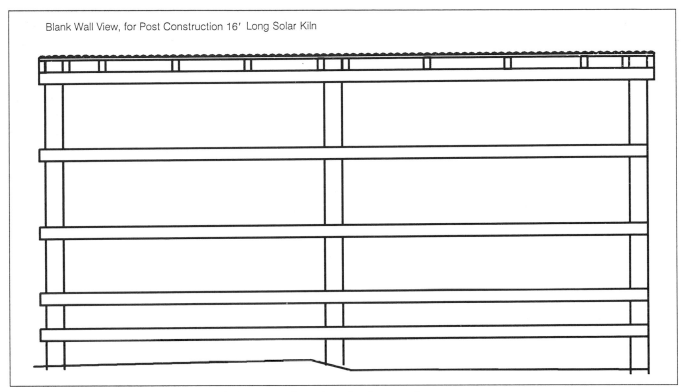

Blank Wall View, for Post Construction 16′ Long Solar Kiln

Rear flat wall. Note the 2 × 4 rafters, on 24-inch centers, do not have fascia or cornice boards applied. The uninterrupted air passage helps drying.

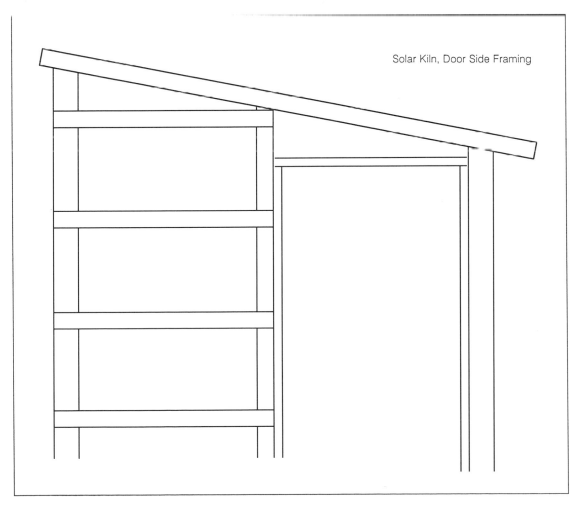

Solar Kiln, Door Side Framing

Use galvanized **T** hinges, at least 6-inch (use three) with 8-inch preferred (use two). Make a drop bar of wood to hold door shut, or use a hook and eye. Door is loosely fitted, again to allow extra air flow that aids drawing by allowing moisture to move outside.

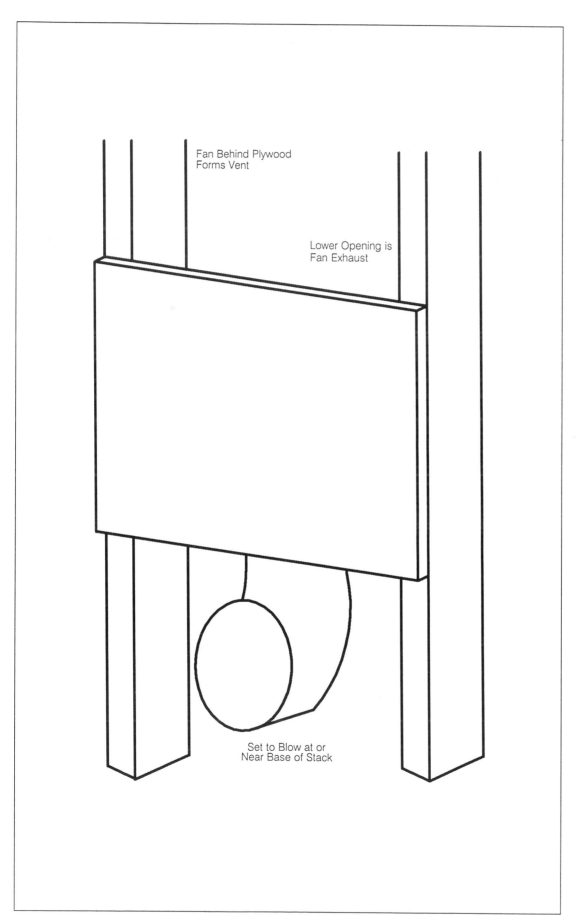

Fan Behind Plywood
Forms Vent

Lower Opening is
Fan Exhaust

Set to Blow at or
Near Base of Stack

Approximate venting for your exhaust fan: You are moving the air under the stacks, cooling it slightly, and it will then gather moisture and rise as it warms, finding its way out at the roof edges and around the door.

in fact), on 24-inch centers. The door is made of ½-inch plywood with 1 × 3 pine framing as a support, and is a full 40 inches wide.

Ventilation

At the front wall (the 8-foot-tall wall, whether you class it front or back, for the other wall is 6 feet tall and covered with clear plastic or glass), install the blower cage design, using a squirrel cage motor to move air from top to bottom of the stack. You may wish to install small fans at the top of the solar wall corners, blowing down on the corners of the stack, to further help air movement. In either instance, small fans are sufficient: You want only a little extra air movement, so that moisture has time to gather in the air being moved. Thus, a 30- to 50-cubic-foot-per-minute fan is sufficient for a moderately large space, such as that in a small solar dryer. A low-end bathroom exhaust fan is almost ideal, if you have trouble locating a small squirrel cage unit. This is the only power the dryer requires, unless you wish to have a light bulb installed. In most areas of the country, you will be able to power the dryer for a full year for about fifteen dollars.

Mount the fan high, and place a plywood or oriented strand board (OSB) cover over the space between two joists, with the bottom left open for about 6 to 8 inches off the floor, so air blows low down, gathers heat and moisture and rises. Point the exhaust side of the fan down when mounting. If you wish, set the wood stickers (on the floor) in a pattern that spreads air under the stack.

If you buy a major brand-name exhaust fan, such as NuTone, you'll find they also sell accessories that make your installation easier, includ-ing programmable switches and all sorts of duct transitions and duct runs. These cost a bit more, but may be worthwhile.

The electrical hookup isn't essential. By allowing more space under the higher roof eave, and by stacking boards on 1½-inch-square stickers, 2 inches apart, you can do without electricity, though the effect on drying must be measured.

The floor, if used, is oriented strand board (OSB) on sawmill 2 × 4s, set on 16-inch centers, which are nailed as joists to sills run 6 inches above the ground (use pressure-treated lumber if you get closer than 6 inches to the ground) inside the vertical members (posts). Lay down at least one layer of 6-mil or heavier black plastic, overlapped 18 inches or more, before laying the floor. Frame interior walls on top of the OSB floor, and right on top of the sills. You'll get the strongest floor and overall assembly if you use 4-inch by ⁵/₁₆-inch or ⅜-inch lag bolts, with appropriate flat washers, one to each junction, plus two 20d nails (coated). Instead of a floor, if you prefer and the site is almost level, lay down *three* layers of 6-mil or heavier black plastic, and level up the floor with clean gravel. Nail roof rafters starting at the outside ends, slanting as required to give a height of 8 feet (total) at the front wall and 6 feet at the back wall (total—from the floor in both cases). Cut the tops of the posts off to match the slant, and do the same at the internal posts, if any. Use 2 × 4 material to lay on eave boards, and nail rafters to these at 24-inch intervals.

Roofing

Over the rafters, every 24 inches up the rafters, lay down and nail nail-ers for the roofing. Apply roofing as recommended by the manufacturer, making sure nothing blocks the corrugations at front or rear (humid air vents at these points).

Place horizontal nailers on the posts, each nailer extending across two posts if more than two are used per side, at 2-foot intervals (vertically). Use 16d or 20d nails, three per junction, to fasten nailers to the posts.

Overall, cover the shed, except for the solar wall, with ½-inch OSB, or with board and batten siding of rough wood (saves money, and allows even more air flow), and lay on a good coat of paint. OSB has waterproof resins, but the wood fibers will swell and change shape if they get wetted too heavily too often. Do not make a tight structure. The whole point is to heat the inside through the solar panels, while allowing, and encouraging, modest air movement at all times.

Leave a space for the door, framed as shown. It's better to frame out a large door: I've spent all the time I want to spend moving boards through small doors that knock the boards, your fingers and anything else in sight. Make the door at an angle to fit the roof, framing it with 1 × 3 or 1 × 4 pine, using construction cement and 8d nails, or 1½-inch staples (and an air stapler).

Again, the door need not fit tightly. In fact, it's best if it doesn't, as that leaves more room for moisture-laden air to escape.

While the specified clear plastic is ultraviolet resistant, it still pays to build the structure so the plastic can be replaced in smaller than overall units. First, a double layer is going to work better under most circumstances than will a single, providing more resistance to wind and to general stretching. The doubling of the material helps build strength to resist wind and impacts, while keeping the span down to a narrower width does the same. Keeping the span down also makes it cheaper to replace sections that get wind-blown and broken, or that get a board shoved through them. Second, the fabric comes in widths particularly suitable to doubling: 36 inches and 48 inches. The 10-mil Flex-O-Pane might be classed as semirigid instead of sheeting, and I'd double that inside and outside of the studs. That is, staple or nail a layer on the inside of the studs, and do the same for another layer on the outside of the studs.

No matter how heavy a non-reinforced plastic material is, you need to provide some kind of barrier to tearing. Furring strips, through which you then staple or nail the material, work nicely. Fit plastic smoothly under a furring strip down one side, and then across the top of the furring strip. Nail or staple in place. Repeat the process for the top, then the bottom and finally, the next side. Do each panel in the same way, which means doubling up the furring strips on vertical wall members (lay one furring strip offset slightly [at least 1 inch on the stud] to finish a plastic panel, and nail in place: Come back and lay the second strip alongside that one, *not* on top of it). Always nail or staple at 12-inch or smaller intervals (stapling is best at 8 inches, while nailing needs to be done at 12 inches) with ring shank nails, and 6 inches with smooth shank nails: Use 1½-inch nails or staples). Where furring strips are not used to prevent tear-through of nailheads in plastic, use a thin strip of heavy cardboard wrapped inside the plastic. Otherwise, the plastic tears too easily, and you'll constantly be replacing the torn panels.

If you have trouble finding material to suit, have your building supply or hardware store call Warp Bros. at (312) 261-5200 and ask for the sales department. It won't do a bit of good to mention my name.

WORKING WITH WOOD

Chapter Eight

MACHINING WOOD

Sears & Roebuck's Craftsman Contractor model jointer is easy to assemble and use, and does an excellent job. The rabbeting ledge is useless because of the way the blades are assembled to the body of the unit: The manual advises against using said ledge, but you can't anyway.

Selecting a jointer is the first step, if you don't already have one. There are a slew of good ones on the market today, including many of the bench types such as Delta's 6-inch variable speed bench jointer, and Ryobi's variable speed, 6⅛-inch, JP155. Both tools are excellent, with the variable speeds allowing easy suiting of jointing, or planing, to the wood type being worked. The JP155 also has a roller set that extends effective table length, while the Delta has a more easily adjusted fence. It's probably a toss-up as to quality: Both are excellent benchtop tools, and do a fine job of edging boards and of light planing of narrower (6 inches and down) stock. Neither has a rabbeting ledge, a loss that isn't pertinent to our immediate needs. As a friend says, for a few months after he first got his jointer, he did all his rabbeting on the jointer, then he went back to using the table saw and router. As a quick note, jointers with rabbeting ledges, like the two following, discourage such use. In fact, Sears's manual says don't do it. The guard must be removed and kickback danger can be rough with a deep cut, so consider carefully if you do attempt rabbeting on a jointer. Myself, 79 percent of the time I use a router, 20 percent of the time a table saw (I never use a radial arm saw for anything approaching a rip cut, and long rabbets run with the grain), and about 1 percent of the time I fool with the jointer. It's a hassle to remove and replace the guard, and it *is* dangerous.

Other jointers include Sears Craftsman's Contractor model, and AMT's massive long-bed jointer, both also 6-inch models (there's not much effective difference between the 6- and 6⅛-inch models). These come with stands and more powerful motors, and do a standard, excellent job of working edges up for almost any use, including glue-ups. Their weight—well, there's a considerable difference between these and the above benchtop models. The AMT is way over 200 pounds, while the Sears Craftsman model is about 150 pounds. Both the Delta and Ryobi jointers are readily delivered by UPS, coming under their maximum weight of 70 pounds.

For light production use (including producing lots of longer lumber with accurately jointed edges), and for contractor use, the stand jointers make more sense. For general shop use, I'm not sure they do, especially when the extra money is added in, but all four of the described models are ones I've recently used exten-

sively, and there isn't one I would chase out of my shop.

I do wish AMT would talk to whoever does the painting of their units: They've got the roughest-looking name plate going. In these days of almost terminal slickness, it's kind of a relief, but I think things might go better if they had that cleaned up a bit. The parts of the machine that do the work, though, are nicely machined, and the castings are suitably heavy. The fence is a tremendous surprise, extending across the center two-thirds of the extra-long table, and offering all sorts of fancy adjustments—but with easy and quick general adjustment.

The Craftsman is lighter and a bit simpler to assemble—yup, you'll end up putting these two tools together, but it's not really that difficult (you do need help getting the motor on the AMT). The Craftsman Contractor model actually requires only the addition of the stand, a pulley and the fence. Both are fine tools.

Using a jointer requires a bit of common sense, and at least two push blocks. There are a multitude of cuts that shouldn't be attempted without push blocks, and your manuals will enlighten you there. Otherwise, use is fairly straightforward when you need to gain a straight edge for glue-up, or from which to work in getting parallel straight edges and on to other types of woodworking. The same jointer techniques work in planing wood 6 inches and narrower: The jointer works well as a dual-purpose tool, and the planer does not.

Jointer Techniques

Basic jointer use is quite simple. Check and see no one is in the kickback area behind the jointer. That's

an area directly behind the jointer, and at least 4 feet wide and 15 feet long. Check to make sure you have necessary push blocks, and goggles or safety glasses. Check your workpiece: The wood must be at least ½-inch thick and 12 inches long, or you cannot safely joint it.

Set the fence inward of the back of the table about an inch, and make sure it is at a 90-degree angle. Each time you reset the fence for positioning, place it an inch or so away from the setting you used last, unless you've been using the entire blade. This evens out the dulling of the blade.

Wear hearing protection, but do *not* wear gloves. Make sure you've removed all jewelry and loose clothing, and keep long hair tied back. The long hair may not be long enough to draw you into the cutters, but it may be long enough to prevent you seeing clearly. Long sleeves must be rolled above the elbow, or tightly buttoned.

Plan hand placement. If you slip, you don't want your hands going into the cutters.

Keep cuts under ¹⁄₁₆ inch when possible.

Of course, make certain there is nothing on the table before you switch on the machine. Later, if material jams or you have other problems, shut the machine off and *unplug* it before clearing the jam or other problem.

The Secret of Jointing Well

Like most other secrets, this one really isn't much more than common sense. Place your feet about shoulder width as you face the machine just to the rear of midpoint, and hold the board firmly down and firmly into the fence. Feed smoothly at a continuous rate of speed that doesn't bog the machine down. Hesitation here causes a skip mark in the edge. When the trailing hand passes over the cutterhead, remove the leading hand, which then goes behind the trailing hand to keep a smooth, continuous feed going. Apply pressure over both cutterhead and outfeed table.

Keep the feed steady and relatively slow. A too-fast feed creates a ripple effect.

If possible, feed with the grain: When against-the-grain feeds cannot be avoided, take very shallow cuts.

Use push blocks when wood narrower than 3 inches and thinner than 3 inches is being planed. If the wood being planed is so narrow the push block is going to tap the jointer cutter guard and move it aside, *tilt* the push block so it misses the guard.

And that's about all there is to basic jointing. From that point, you can move on to the types of jointing that aren't a part of this book, things like beveling and cutting taper angles on legs, and all sorts of things that you might figure can't be done without a lot of special machinery. The jointer is a shop essential, and is more useful than many woodworkers give it credit for being.

Set fence, carefully, at 90 degrees.

USING THE PLANER

Ryobi's introduction of the AP10 portable planer some years ago gave the home shop woodworker a second choice: The original low-cost planer, the 12-inch Shopsmith, cost close to $900 at the time, and the little Ryobi came in, discounted, under $400, a considerable drop. Suddenly, planers were a rational tool for the serious woodworker who didn't want to go bankrupt. Back then, the Shopsmith had been the bottom step on a flight of stairs with

Bobby Weaver is properly dressed for jointing, with hearing protection and eye protection. Note that long sleeves are buttoned.

Hand placement is correct — and correct placement can save fingers.

the next stop at around $1,500, where it remains today for a larger, stationary planer. Simply put, not many of us can afford that kind of money for a single tool.

The AP10 has gone, replaced by the AP12, a 12⁵⁄₁₆-inch planer with quickly changed blades. Makita's 12-inch version was the first competition that forced Ryobi larger, but they were quickly followed by Penn State, Sears Craftsman, Grizzly, Reliant, Sunhill, Wilke, Jet and Hitachi. After discounts, prices may range down from the Hitachi's $700-plus to as little as $370 for the Sunhill. Most are in the $400 range, or just under. You may still find a few of the Ryobi AP10s around for prices under $350.

Ryobi and Makita probably have the easiest-to-change blades, which are disposable. Every single one of these small planers offers superb smoothness of cut, almost a silky feel to the wood (depending on species) when it's cut. I've used a large number of them, but not all, so I can't state more than a minor preference for the Makita, Ryobi and Delta.

Snipe is a problem with all of the small planers. Snipe is a cupped cut near the end of boards as they come out of the planer. This can be reduced, but cannot be eliminated in these planers.

These are not production planers. I got a bit too far into planing some oak one day a few years ago and destroyed the drive belt on my Makita. This isn't a major problem, except that changing the belt does not come under the heading of fun. Too much heat will ruin drive belts and other parts on these machines fairly quickly, but if given a half-hour break after an hour's planing, the machines serve long and well.

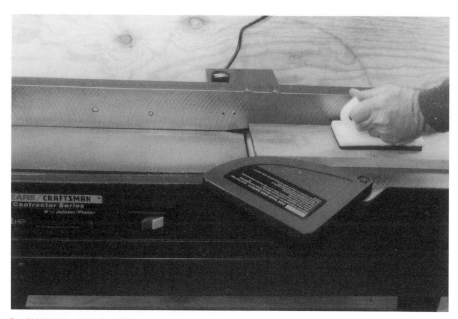

Push blocks make flat planing much safer — all jointers are delivered with at least one push block, but a pair is essential.

Make sure the blade guard swings open and closed readily and with little resistance.

Planer Techniques

Effective planing requires several things. Start with properly dried wood and a ready-to-go planer. From there, add in dust protection for yourself and anyone around: The mass of shavings and dust produced in planing even 100 board feet is hard to believe. Make sure you've got support for boards both going in — your job? — and coming out —

outfeed table or an alert helper. Take fairly shallow cuts, and butt boards one behind the other as you feed them into the planer. Keeping cuts shallow, butting boards and supporting boards all help to reduce snipe. In the end, snipe is best handled by adding 4 or 5 inches to the length of the boards needed.

When working on cupped, twisted or warped stock, flatten it on the

Ryobi's 12-inch planer is a wonder, plowing its way through thick and thin.

jointer first. Small planers use less infeed pressure on wood, so are less likely to force cup or warp out of a board as it is planed, allowing it to pop back in after it passes the blades, but jointers still do a better job of eliminating problems with badly shaped stock.

Naturally, you also want to make sure your knives are sharp. As with a jointer, vary the feed spot of narrow boards so knives dull evenly across their entire width. Run the boards through only with the grain: Planers are not designed to handle cross-grain work.

WORKING WITH HIGHLY FIGURED WOODS AND BURLS

Feed burl and similar highly figured stock at an angle to reduce tear-out. A better solution to tear-out with highly figured woods is to find someone with a sanding planer, and use that to surface fancier stock. There are a number of such units around, including one that mounts on a radial arm saw and gives an incredible width, and all are said to work from reasonably well on up to superla-

tively. Prices for stand-alone units tend to approximate the prices for 15-inch-width planers, so they're not cheap, though the radial arm saw unit is much less costly than others.

BONDING WOOD

The world's greatest wood isn't worth much if you can't put the pieces together to form some sort of coherent whole. Thus, you must be able to join woods using common, or nearly common, bonding methods and materials. In most cases, domestic softwoods and hardwoods bond at worst satisfactorily, and in most cases well or easily. The only two domestic woods I know of that create major bonding difficulties are osage orange and persimmon, both of which may be readily bonded using the same techniques one uses for any difficult-to-bond wood, such as teak. That is, clean the mating surfaces with alcohol or other solvent, and apply one of the new wood epoxies.

Woods that bond easily are: Alder; Aspen; Basswood; Cottonwood; Chestnut; Magnolia; Willow, black; Fir, white, grand, noble, Pa-

cific; Pine, Eastern white, Western white; Red cedar, Western; Redwood; Spruce, Sitka; Balsa; Purpleheart.

Woods that bond well are: Butternut; Elm, American and rock; Hackberry; Maple, soft; Sweetgum; Sycamore; Tupelo; Walnut, black; Yellow poplar; Douglas fir; Larch, Western; Pine, sugar, ponderosa, red cedar, Eastern; Andiroba; Angelique; Avodire; Jarrah; Mahogany, African and American; Meranti (lauan); Obeche.

Woods that bond satisfactorily are: Ash, white; Beech, American; Birch, sweet and yellow; Cherry; Hickory, pecan and true; Maple, hard; Oak, red and white; Alaska cedar; Port Orford cedar; Pine, Southern; Benge; Bubinga; Ramin.

Woods that bond with difficulty are: Osage orange; Persimmon; Greenheart; Lignum vitae; Rosewood; Teak.

Wood Glues and Adhesives

The primary use of wood glues is to hold joints together. There are other applications, but the major use is making strong wood joints in furniture and other assemblies. Proper gluing will relieve some of the internal stresses of wood, particularly in laminating flat boards and reducing warping, cupping, and other forms of distortion. Too, adhesives allow us to use many parts of a board that are otherwise pieces of scrap, letting us make wide boards from narrow, thick from thin and so on.

There aren't as many true woodworking glues as you may be led to believe, but there is a wide enough variety to cover the storage-project maker's need for strong joints. And there's a new, inexpensive, weatherproof glue, Titebond II, from Franklin International. Woodworking adhesives are classed as animal or hide glues and synthetics.

Hide Glues

Hide, or animal, glues come from boiling down hides, hoofs and bones of animals to produce glue. The most common liquid hide glue today is Franklin's. The glue is nontoxic. Its slow drying time gives a nice, long assembly time which is superb for complex projects, allowing adjustments and changes that can't be made with faster-setting glues.

Hide glues are thicker than white or yellow synthetic glues, resist solvents (except water) well, and leave a pale tan glue line. They sand nicely, without gumming. Lack of gumming is important, because glues that gum heavily clog and ruin sandpaper quickly. Hide glues resist water poorly.

Dry hide glue is available, but mostly it makes sense to use liquid hide glue. Dry hide glue is mixed with water and heated, and then held at 140 to 150°. You must first soak the granules in cold water. They soften after several hours, and you pour off excess water. Then you heat the glue, and hold the temperature while the glue is stirred smooth and lump free.

Apply hot hide glue with a stiff brush, and clamp the joint while the glue is still hot. The wood must be warmed to at least 70° in cold shops. Neither the wood nor the glue should be overheated; too much heat cuts strength.

Liquid hide glue is simpler to use—it's spread normally, without heating, and still gives a long assembly time when that's needed. I'd suggest using it for some of your projects: It's a handy glue, and getting

familiar with it is a lot of fun.

For most of woodworking history, hide glue was the epitome of wood-joining strength. It is still sometimes considered tops, but comes with multiple problems. Still, hide glue has many advantages, and continues to be good for some jobs.

In summary: *Hide glues present slow drying, low—very low—moisture resistance (which is good in many situations), an attractive glue line, excellent strength, long clamping time, long open time, and generally difficult setup and working with the dried glues. Liquid hide glues remove much of the difficulty, and retain many of the other good features. Sandability is excellent for both.*

Synthetic Adhesives

By far the greatest percentage of woodworking adhesives are synthetics, made especially for use in woodworking. Some come from other fields. Most are resin glues that gather strength by chemical reaction, or curing. Curing depends on the temperature of the glue. Strength of cure and speed of set increase with rising glue temperature, but heating too much isn't wise. Maximum cure temperature is about 110° for yellow (aliphatic) resin glue, while others do best at a low 75 to 80°.

Polyvinyl Acetate Resins

White glues (polyvinyl acetate resins) come ready to use in squeeze bottles on up to gallon and larger jugs. There are many brands acceptable for general woodworking purposes.

White glues use a water move cure: Water in the glue moves into the wood and the air, and the resin then gels. On unstressed joints, you

can release clamping pressure inside of forty-five minutes, but leaving clamping pressure on for several hours is better. Stressed joints must set for six hours before clamp release. Some white glues are dyed yellow and some tan to appear more like aliphatic resin glues. Aliphatic resin glues resist heat and water better than do white glues.

Low heat resistance means poor sanding qualities. Glue softens because of heat generated during sanding, gumming up the sandpaper. Low heat resistance also causes loss of glue strength at 100° and up. Water resistance is also low in white glue.

White glue set is quick, cutting assembly time to ten minutes. Pressure application has to be fast, so projects must be test-assembled. Fit all clamps to a half turn before disassembling. Apply adhesive, and reassemble for clamping. Clamp quickly, with medium pressure.

The glue line is almost transparent when white glue has dried. In a cold shop (under 70°) the glue will be a chalky white, and the joint line is weak.

White glue gives with day-to-day movement of the wood, a process known as cold flow, so it is not useful for highly stressed joints. Cold flow lets joints move without creating cracked glue lines and weakening low-stressed joints, so white glue is good for those project joints.

In summary: *White glue is a good, inexpensive glue that requires speed in assembly and clamping, and gums up sandpaper during sanding. Poor heat resistance means white glues are best not used during hot summer days. Glue line is almost invisible.*

Liquid Yellow Glues (Aliphatic Resin)

Aliphatic resin glues were designed as improvements over polyvinyl resin glues. Heat resistance is better, upgrading sandability while improving joint strength at 100° and up. Yellow glues set well at temperatures up to 110°, which means they can be used on hot summer days. Assembly is easier at low temperatures; raising the glue temperature speeds set rate and reduces open time. The glue line is a translucent pale tan or amber color.

Yellow glues are thicker and heavier than white glues, making them neater to use. Greater moisture resistance means you can glue projects for use in most damp basements.

Unfortunately, set is even faster than for white glues, a problem if you are assembling complex storage projects. Switch to hide glue when project assembly is going to need more than five or ten minutes.

Total cure for yellow glue is twenty-four hours. Water cleans up before the glue sets.

In summary: Yellow glue is an excellent general purpose glue, best suited to small projects because of fast set time. Test-assemble all projects, and set up larger projects for assembly in modules to use this type of glue. Does not gum sandpaper. Resists heat and moderate dampness well. It is not waterproof, not even truly water resistant.

A yellow glue, Titebond II wood glue is a new heat-resistant, weatherproof resin glue that is sufficiently waterproof to be used everywhere but below water lines. It is similar in joint appearance to other yellow glues, but sets even more rapidly—I have to wonder if the chemists can adjust this to give those of us who are clumsy a bit more time. Initial tack is strong, set is fast (about five minutes!), and it does not gum badly during sanding. Clamp for about one half hour. It is a bit more temperature critical, at least on the cold side, than are regular resin glues: I used it in two projects that had chalky-appearing excess glue when shop temperatures were below about 60° F.

Titebond II is only modestly more expensive than standard Titebond, does the same work, and adds the bonus of being waterproof. It is now my basic shop glue.

Waterproof and Water-Resistant Glues

Plastic resin adhesives are highly water resistant, but the resorcinols (and epoxies) are truly waterproof. It's a lot cheaper to use plastic resins or the earlier described Titebond II when you can.

Resorcinol resin glues are dark red liquid resins with which a catalytic powder is mixed before use. Resorcinols have a reasonable working time, from about a quarter of an hour to two hours. Check the labels first to suit your working style.

Before starting, make sure wood moisture content is below 12 percent, joints are tight, and heavy-duty clamps are on hand. Brush resorcinol on or spread with a spatula. Tongue depressors, from any drugstore, make fine glue spreaders, as do ice cream sticks from the grocery store, and toothpicks for small projects.

When dense hardwoods are glued, make sure there is no lack of glue—glue starvation—in tight-fitting joints. Coat both surfaces lightly, and leave the joint open for the maximum time before clamping. Increasing shop temperature helps to make sure the glue gets where it's needed.

Clamping pressure is high, 200 pounds per square inch. The pressure has to be uniform which means clamps spaced more closely.

The glue line is ugly, a dark red or reddish brown.

In summary: Resorcinol resin glue is a difficult-to-use, obstinate glue that has an ugly glue line, but that offers superb working time, and a totally waterproof joint. Keep it warm during use (above 70°, preferably close to 80). You must have a tight joint to start with because resorcinol has poor gap-filling qualities. (Use epoxy for sloppy joints that must be waterproof.)

Plastic Resin Adhesives

Plastic resin adhesives are dry powders, mixed with water just before use. The resin is urea formaldehyde, a highly water-resistant adhesive, best used on wood with a moisture content of no more than 12 percent. Best use and cure temperature is 70°.

Plastic resin glues are for projects that must take long-term dampness. They are good general-purpose glues, working easily, except with high-density woods such as maple and oak. Precise fit of joints is needed—plastic resin glues are not good gap fillers.

Glue set is affected by temperature, so leave complex assembly jobs to cooler hours or do in air-conditioned areas. Working life ranges from one to five hours. Clamp pressure of nine hours, up to twelve, is needed. Clamps are taken off when squeeze-out is hard. Clamp pressure is moderate.

In summary: *The glue line of plastic resin adhesives is a light tan color. Gumming is not a problem as the resin resists heat well; general working is easy, and mixing from powder is quick and simple. Yellow glues are used because they are ready-mix, and the fast set is a help on many projects, but urea resin glues are as good or better in most areas, though less convenient.*

Epoxy Adhesives

Epoxies aren't handy for most projects, but new formulas have been developed that do aid woodworking use of these adhesives. Some years ago epoxies were almost *no* use around the small woodshop. They were useful for repairs and useless for most other purposes. Now, cost, toxicity and mess are the limiting factors.

Epoxies are two-part adhesives, a liquid hardener that is added to a liquid resin. Cure is by chemical reaction. Heat is produced during the reaction.

Mix only as much as you will use immediately. Epoxies are costly.

When using a wood such as teak, epoxies simplify matters. They are made to fit about any bonding need in moderate temperature applications.

Set time is important in wood adhesives. One of the reasons epoxies missed early popularity was that most are fast-set types, under five minutes. Such speed is fine for many things, including very small woodworking projects and repairs, but causes a problem on larger projects.

Epoxies are very toxic, limiting

uses in some shops. They are also messy, a problem easily solved. Wear thin plastic gloves, available in packs of 100, to avoid the hand mess. Clean up quickly with acetone (if you can't find acetone, get nail polish remover), keeping the gloves on. Make sure all mixing containers and sticks are disposable.

Working with dense woods or with exotics such as rosewood, teak and ebony, you have no other choice. Epoxy is it. Clamping pressure is light, working time is adjustable, to as much as ninety minutes, gap filling is superb, strength is incredible, and the resulting glue line is either clear or an amber color.

In summary: *Epoxy doesn't shrink, so it is a good gap filler. Some is formed as putty for filling huge gaps, though tight joint fits are still better for long project life. Glue line is clear, and it has good heat resistance and is impervious to water and most chemicals. It is expensive, hard to use, and may present fume problems if used in large amounts.*

Contact Cements

Contact cements are useful when you work with wood composite substrates such as fiberboard. Contact cement may go over almost any wood substrate, but works best over composites that are more stable dimensionally, so that the plastic laminate cemented over the top remains in place. Some wood laminates—veneers—may be placed with contact cement, though traditionally hide glue is more popular. Wood substrates may be plywood, or one of the formed boards. The latter are usually best because, over the years, plywood grains may start to show

through the plastic laminates.

Contact cements come in two basic types. One uses a water solvent, while the other uses another non-flammable solvent base. UGL's Safe Grip uses nonflammable 111 Trichloroethane as the solvent. Avoid professional types that use flammable solvents.

Vapors are harmful even with newer solvents: Make sure you work with proper ventilation. Some water-based solvents are also pretty rough on the lungs. A few may not be safe around an open flame. Check before using any of them. Do not use flammable contact cements.

Contact cements give a quick bond with cleanup and trim of the final project possible immediately. Use is simple. Coat both surfaces with the cement, using a brush or a roller. Let the surfaces dry (to the touch: The cement will appear clear). Place laminate on the substrate.

Make sure the laminate is positioned correctly over the wood. A slip sheet of kraft paper or waxed paper may be used, covering the entire adhesive surface. Leave enough paper to grip outside the two pieces being joined. Bring the top piece down, align the two pieces, and slowly start slipping the paper out. Once the paper is out 3 inches, roll or tap over the cleared area to assure a bond. Pull the paper the rest of the way out, using care not to disturb alignment. Roll or tap the laminate surface to make a solid bond.

Instead of a slip sheet, you can use ¾-inch-square wood stickers at intervals. Placing stickers across the full width of the base material works well at 1-inch or smaller intervals. Lay the adhesive-coated laminate on the stickers and align. Start sticker removal at the center sticker so laminate sags and touches the base material coating. Tap or roll, and remove the remaining stickers, tapping and rolling as you go.

In summary: *Contact cements do not provide a visible glue line, and the cement is not made to be sanded, so those features are not covered. Bond is strong, within intended uses, which are limited to bonding sheet material (Micarta and similar laminated plastic sheets; veneers) to a substrate of manufactured wood such as plywood. Limited working time, but usually more than sufficient. Requires care, but works well. Cleanup is usually easy with water-based versions, and not extremely difficult with those based on other solvents. Never use flammable contact cements.*

Choosing Glues

Selection of glue is important, but so are application and clamping of parts. Also important is working with a tight-fitting joint so there are no gap-filling problems or joints weakened by thick expanses of nothing but glue.

Make any glue selection on the qualities your project needs most. My listing isn't all-encompassing, but it's complete enough for almost all woodworkers. If assembly is complicated and time-consuming, and moisture is no problem, use hide glue. If moisture is a moderate problem, pick a urea resin glue instead of yellow glue.

For general uses, liquid yellow glues and polyvinyl acetate (white resin) glues are best. Pick white glue for longer assembly times, and yellow glue for better moisture resistance, better sanding and thicker spreading qualities that give better gap filling.

For water resistance, choose Titebond II, epoxy or urea resin—urea resin or Titebond II first, unless the epoxies fill some other specific need such as great unsupported strength or gap filling. Epoxies are too costly for general use.

For total waterproofing, use resorcinol. Expensive and difficult to apply properly, resorcinol takes very precise-fitting joints, and leaves an ugly glue line, but is completely impervious to water.

The type of glue chosen determines method of application, though most may be applied with a brush, stick or roller. Joint surfaces first must be checked. If the joint surface is a tight fit, clean off all dust, oil, old glue, loosened and torn grain and chips. Any machining (cutting) of wood that has to be done is done as close as possible to the time of gluing and assembly.

A test assembly is a good idea—once glue is added, correcting mistakes is messy. If mistakes creep in and glue sets, mistakes stay.

Before you apply the glue, test assemble to see whether the unit can be assembled within the time required. If a glue has a ten-minute open time, assembly must be completed within that time limit. The thicker the glue you spread, generally, the longer the open assembly time. If wood is very porous or dry, open assembly time decreases.

If the test assembly takes more than the allotted time, change the method of gluing or the type of adhesive used so there's enough time to complete and clamp the assembly. Mix all adhesives according to the maker's directions, and as accurately as possible. Spread evenly over the surfaces to be joined.

PEG

If PEG sounds more familiar when I call it polyethylene glycol, that's because most of the automobiles in the world cart around a solution of the stuff in their radiators. It's also known as antifreeze, in other words. PEG for woodworkers is different in that it comes in solid, bulk form, and can be bought by the pound. As sold through The Woodworkers' Store, it is a blob of white, waxy-looking material in a plastic bucket. There are other differences than color and nonliquid state: PEG is not listed as a poisonous material, while automobile polyethylene glycol most assuredly is. I don't know, though, if that's a characteristic of the PEG, or the dye, or another chemical added to prevent rust, lubricate the various auto internals or what, so I'd suggest using care when working with PEG. Always store PEG where pets and children cannot get to it. Better safe than sorry.

PEG is a fast treatment for green lumber, and is probably best used when you carve or turn an object from green wood, and want to keep it from checking and cracking and generally falling apart as the wood dries.

PEG replaces water molecules in the cellular structure of the wood, and then does not evaporate, so the wood becomes stable. The process by which it does this is unimportant to us here, but we do need to know that PEG will not penetrate more than about 2 inches of wood from any direction. This limits project thicknesses to about 4 inches, with 2 inches being more practical.

Treatment is affected by wood

density. PEG works best with low and medium density woods. In fact, it doesn't work at all with heartwood from hard maple and white oak. You've got to season those the hard way, over time.

PEG is used in plastic containers. Contact with metals should be minimum to none, so a good source of small barrels or waste baskets or similar products will be handy. PEG is seldom used on enough wood to do a large project, as it does tend to run up project cost, though you can make quite large temporary treatment vats by lining wood troughs with 6-mil plastic, backed by enough sand to pack corners, to keep solution use down. Currently, PEG will cost you about five dollars a pound, delivered. A 10-pound bucket can be used to make 15.4 quarts of 30 percent solution, or 8.5 quarts of 50 percent solution. The stronger solution does a quicker job of stabilizing the wood.

You can start with 10 pounds of PEG and easily know what solution strength you are using, but as time passes water evaporates, so you lose track of solution strength, especially when you must add water. Using a hydrometer, the 30 percent solution measures 1.05 at 60° F, and the 50 percent solution measures 1.093 at the same temperature. Keep them close to those figures, and you can get many, many uses out of your original 10 pounds of chemical. To check specific gravity, cool small amounts of the solution down to 60° F in the fridge or freezer.

Oddly enough, PEG works a great deal better if wood is very wet when treatment starts. With more moisture in the cell structure, more PEG displaces it, giving better stability, faster. If worse comes to worse,

soak your project for a week or two before stabilizing it with PEG! It really works better that way.

Most projects are best treated in intermediate stages. That is, work the project to within about ½-inch of its final shape, and then treat it.

PEG presents you with easy-to-work wood, right up until you have to sand the stuff. PEG-treated wood clogs sandpaper in a rush, so use either an open-coat sandpaper, or wet and dry sandpaper, using water as a lubricant.

Finishing can present some problems, but nothing insurmountable. Danish oil finishes work well, and lightly treated projects, such as bowls, may be finished with regular polyurethanes. Epoxy finishes also work well. Finishes that provide a noninterrupted final coat are best, so that water vapor cannot pass through and settle on the wood.

SELECTING WOOD FOR PROJECTS

Making successful wood projects, whether a single project or a dozen different projects (or one project a dozen different times) means using an appropriate adhesive and correct clamping, and allowing plenty of drying time. Woods to be joined must mate well: Too much difference in wood structure or moisture content creates problems. Teak, for example, with its high silicone and oil contents, does not bond well with any other wood. It is often difficult to bond to itself, thus always needs one of the top-grade epoxies.

Using the same species of wood gives the best results, the longest and strongest hold. If all boards in a project are pine or fir or oak or cherry, all is fine. If one is cherry and another pine, difficulties arise.

When using different species, use them in sections where glue is not needed. Cabinet door making is an example: The inner panel floats loose in the stiles and rails. The glued-up inner panel may be of any species, with stiles and rails of a different species. Because the sections are not firmly joined, there are no glue joint problems.

Also, use plainsawn boards with plainsawn boards, and quartersawn boards with quartersawn. Otherwise, differences in grain directions create wood distortion.

Leave boards at least twenty-four hours in the environment in which they will be glued. Several days is better. This allows the boards to "temper," or stabilize, internally so immediate movement is reduced, and later movement is matching, or close to it.

Wood seems an innocuous material unless you surround yourself with it and set it on fire. But that's not always so: Wood isn't extremely harmful, but can cause respiratory and skin problems of varying degrees of severity, depending on wood species and your personal susceptibility to the allergens in the material.

Different times can create different effects. Some years ago, I was hanging a sign—wood, of course—on an old cedar tree. In the process, I managed to stick a toe part way into a yellow jacket nest at the base of the tree (at the time, I had no idea such areas were favored wasp breeding grounds). For one of the few times in my life, I was wearing shorts and a T-shirt, and got stung seven times before I ran out of range.

Not a real problem, if painful. Some Benadryl, some rest, and a chance to sand a mahogany desk I was refinishing. And that was a mistake. Within a few hours, I was a mass of hives and getting worse, so I made my way to the doctor's office, where a couple of shots almost immediately relieved the problem.

Part way, and for a short time. About 1 A.M. the problem returned, in greater force, and the swelling was starting to cramp my throat muscles, so a trip to the emergency room was in order for more needlework.

What the problem turned out to be was a combination of two things, a substance (mahogany) to which I was mildly allergic, and a sensitizer (any one, or all seven stings from those miserable flying insects). The result was a big mess.

The use of care in associating items helps, of course: If you're working with woods that are possibly allergenic, or heavily so, it pays to avoid chances of bee sting, extra booze, and a slew of other minutiae that might push reactions over the edge. Believe me, it's best to avoid the reactions!

It also helps to have an idea of what woods are apt to give you a kick and what woods aren't, while remembering that all dust can create problems, not necessarily allergy related. Dust in the lung sacs is bad for you. Period. When doing heavy sanding, sawing, planing, jointing, or generally working with wood of any kind, a decent dust mask is a good idea, as is hearing protection when working with most power tools (but especially with planers, jointers, shapers and routers).

Because toxic substances do inhabit most woods, and some may be carcinogens, it *always* pays to wear a dust mask. A decent dust collection system, or frequent vacuuming, can be helpful in preventing problems in a small shop, with preference going to dust collection, if it's done right.

Generally, you're figured to have about one chance in a hundred of having problems from toxicity in wood. You can knock those odds on the head with a few steps:

• Ventilate for air flow and coolness, to limit dust-collecting perspiration.

• Run your dust collection system or wear your Fed-approved dust mask (look for the statement that it's approved by the National Institute for Occupational Safety and Health).

• Wear a long-sleeved shirt with tight cuffs and collar.

• When working with rough woods, wear tight-fitting gloves. I generally hate wearing gloves of any kind, but have found the tight goatskin Grips gloves from Wells-Lamont (model 1770), and Leichtung's tight, always-on-sale threefers (three pairs for a special price, which is always low but too variable to give here) are excellent. When working with near-finished woods, I prefer to wash more frequently, which, anyway, comes next.

• Shower thoroughly at the end of all woodworking sessions, even if it works out to two or three showers a day. One of the problems I had when I got stung and reacted was a lack of showering facilities: The house we were renting had only a huge old clawfoot bathtub, which is great for comfort but doesn't help you clean up as well as a plain old shower.

• Remember that woods are divided into two classes, irritants and sensitizers, but that events may well create irritants from woods that are normally sensitizers (my experience with mahogany).

Some woods are dangerous enough to be deadly, and it is felt that tannin dust may well be carcinogenic

(cancer-causing). Evidently, the disease formed from tannin has an exceptionally long—forty years or more—gestation period, making it difficult to tell for sure if it's the causative substance.

Woods that are irritants cause contact dermatitis, and will cause the reactions in just about everyone if the wood is handled long enough. The major symptom will be a rash; that rash may erupt into blisters and may not. In my case it was hives, and the wood was really a sensitizer, but circumstances had already sensitized me, so it became a primary irritant and created some larger problems. Otherwise, sensitizers tend to affect only those people who are allergic to that specific wood, or family of woods. The effects from sensitizers are seldom as severe as those from primary irritants, but other complicating factors in your personal history may make them so.

Sensitizers cause swelling and symptoms similar to those of asthma. Constant exposure over time may cause contact dermatitis. It is said that no wood is known to cause respiratory problems, but cancer is a problem created by dust, and is often of the nasal sinuses. Too, my case of hives was becoming a respiratory problem when the swelling threatened to close my throat. So these allergies are seldom anything to fool with, as mild as most of them are.

Always be sure to let any doctor know you're a woodworker if you must make a visit because of allergic symptoms. If cancer comes from woods with high tannin contents, we especially need to behave ourselves around oaks, redwood, Western red cedar and hemlocks.

You can control some factors when you're harvesting your own wood. Using only heartwood reduces problems, because most of the toxic substances are in leaves and stems, then the bark, next the sapwood, and last, the heartwood.

Try to do your cutting in the tree's dormant season, fall and winter, for wood is more toxic when the sap is flowing in the tree as it is cut.

Season the wood well before using. Green wood causes more reactions, but not because it is more toxic. Sawdust from green wood sticks because it is damp; thus it deposits more of the toxins because it is around longer.

Don't use wood from toxic species for food-contact projects or for jewelry.

If symptoms show up, and persist, after using wood (symptoms may not materialize for a dozen or so hours), get in touch with your doctor, a dermatologist or allergist.

Checking the following list will give you the basis for avoiding woods that seem likely to interact with medications or habits. For further information, check with your doctor or a dermatologist. The list is not complete by any means, and only indicates whether a wood is an irritant or a sensitizer.

WOOD SENSITIVITY TABLE

Wood Species	Primary Irritant	Sensitizer
Bald cypress		x
Balsam fir		x
Beech		x
Black locust	x	
Boxwood		x
Cocobolo	x	
Ebony	x	
Elm		x
Goncalo alves		x
Greenheart		x
Hemlock		x (probable extreme carcinogen)
Mahogany		x
Maple		x
Mimosa (junk wood, but everywhere)	x	
Oak, red		x (probable carcinogen)
Olivewood		x
Padauk	x	
Purpleheart		x
Redwood		x (probable carcinogen)
Rosewood		x
Satinwood	x	
Sassafras		x
Sequoia	x	
Snakewood	x	
Spruce		x
Walnut		x
Wenge		x
Willow		x
Western red cedar		x
Teak		x
Yew, European	x	

Chapter Nine

MANUFACTURED WOOD

Manufacturing plywood.
Courtesy of Georgia-Pacific Corporation.

ou may wonder a bit about what a chapter on manufactured woods is doing in a book on producing your own wood: It is a step to further saving money when building projects. As with softwoods and hardwoods, if you know what to look for when buying softwood or hardwood plywoods and structural panels, you can save a considerable amount of money when setting up to build many projects.

Overall, the purpose of this book is to save you money, and this chapter is aimed at continuing the process. We'll look at different plywoods, OSB, hardboards and similar products, and see what is available on today's market, within what classifications. It's possible to do a better job, and save money, with plywoods, though often plywood is not really cheaper than solid wood. Plywood, though, may be easier to work, and it may produce a better-looking project that serves longer with fewer problems because plywood is more dimensionally stable than solid wood.

For those woodworkers who say plywood doesn't suit their idea of solid wood, nor does it suit mine — but furniture manufacturers now class it that way. However, plywood does suit my idea of a product that serves a multiplicity of purposes, some very well, others well, and some not so well. And please, no complaints that plywood is a modern material, and thus no good. Plywood is a stack of veneer plies. Most top-quality older furniture used veneers on wide panels — often for the very same reasons we use plywood in wide panels today. The substrate

doesn't have to be fancy, nor does it have to be expensive, but the final layer can be gorgeous, making the entire piece lovely to look at — and to use. Marquetry, the application of small patterns in a larger surface, isn't the only use for veneers, and never has been. There is no other way to apply burl patterns to a project, at least that is practical.

While pressure-treated woods aren't essential for very many wood-worker's projects, they do turn up with some frequency as adjuncts to those projects, such as poles for birdhouses and feeders, poles for pole structures, landscaping timbers to support stacks of lumber and for similar uses. Pressure-treated woods are also useful in noncontact areas of outdoor projects, such as roofs on birdhouses and feeders, garden furniture projects, etc.

Plywood coming off the line is checked.
Courtesy of Georgia-Pacific Corporation.

So, into the wide world of ply-woods we go, with an emphasis on those of greatest use to the widest number of woodworkers.

PLYWOOD

Plywood gets better in slow steps, and was more than pretty good by the time World War II PT boats were made of the layered substance. Whether hardwood or softwood, plywood is usually made up of an odd number of plies (please note the *usually*: A very few rare types of hardwood plywood offer even numbers of plies). Face plies have the grain running the long way of the panel, and intermediate plies in opposing directions (the reason for the odd number of plies). The fact that the plies run in differing directions makes plywood both stronger and more dimensionally stable than solid wood of the same species and with the same thickness.

The dimensional stability is what makes plywood such a great wood for woodworkers: You can make very wide panel faces serve as room and cabinet paneling, tables and desktops, and use it in all sorts of other jobs without having to worry about warping and cupping.

Plywood also makes marvelous backs, sides and bottoms for desks and cabinets and other projects where those sections are not seen. It may also be used as a substrate for laminates (underlayment, essentially) and veneers.

Softwood Plywood

Softwood plywood is both a supporting and a leading material for many woodworking projects, and as such is a good component to check for savings. There are enough variations in this material that a discussion

of all of them would keep you reading for hours, so I'm going to explain only those of importance in woodworking—though that includes OSB and some similar materials also used in different areas.

Face grades start with N, for natural finishes, and go on down to D, used as a backup grade only, for CDX and other panels, and for interior plies. I'm not going to detail what's legal by American Plywood Association standards in all grades of softwood plywood, though I'll list the general requirements. You can often tell grades by a simple glance at the faces. For example, CDX is a rough grade, meant totally for sheathing and similar uses; the clean face is backed by the not-so-clean (in terms of gaps, etc.) and Exterior glue is used (the X). It is obvious at a glance if you have any experience with plywood at all, but, as with all APA-graded plywood, it will be stamped with grade uses, as well as span allowances for the particular thickness of the panel.

Softwood Plywood Grades

First, we have N grade. *Grade N* softwood plywood panels are intended for natural finishes, so they are smoothly cut of 100 percent heartwood or 100 percent sapwood, and must be free of knotholes, pitch pockets, open splits and other open defects, and stains. The panels in 48-inch widths cannot be made up of more than two pieces, while wider panels can go to three. Synthetic fillers may be used in cracks and checks $\frac{1}{32}$ inch and narrower, and in small splits no more than $\frac{1}{16}$ inch wide and 2 inches long. Faces are limited to a total of six, and must be well matched for grain and color. This is the top-grade softwood plywood panel, and should be bought only when it is the primary part of the project. The project is finished with clear materials over a stain, or it can be done without a stain.

More frequently, plywood projects call for a coat of paint, and that's where *Grade A* plywood comes in. The veneer must be smooth and firm, and free of knots, pitch pockets, open splits and open defects. Synthetic fillers may be used to fill cracks and checks to $\frac{1}{32}$ inch wide, and small splits to $\frac{1}{16}$ inch wide and 2 inches long. On Interior panels, small cracks or checks may be as much as $\frac{3}{16}$ inch wide by 2 inches long when filled, and depressions to $\frac{1}{2}$ inch by 2 inches may also be filled. Patches are limited to 18 in number, parallel to grain, and each shall not be more than $2\frac{1}{4}$ inches in width.

The panel I prefer for paint is *Grade B*. It is more roughly sanded than A grade, but is also lower in cost. The veneer should be solid and free of open defects and broken grain, except as listed below. Slightly rough grain is allowed. Minor sanding and patching defects, including sander skips, must not exceed 5 percent of the panel area. Small splits and checks, and chipped areas as in A grade Exterior panels can be filled. In Interior panels, cracks and checks may be larger, as in A grade. Knots are allowed but can't be larger than 1 inch, and must be sound and tight. Pitch streaks over an inch in width are not allowed. Splits to 1/32 inch may be left open, as may vertical holes up to 1/16 inch in diameter. The holes shall not exceed one per square foot in number. All in all, this panel takes more work to ready for the paint can or spray gun, but the savings over A grade can be considerable. If A is affordable, go with it, but if the project completion hinges on a matter of dollars, grab B grade, a random orbit sander (one of the brands with more than 3 amperes of power for this work) and sanding discs in 80 and 120 grit, plus a pint or so of top-quality wood filler.

Random orbit sanders are the current marvel of the woodworking world, and deservedly so, as they do a fantastic job of removing excess wood while leaving a very smooth, swirl-free surface for finish. The more powerful brands take off almost as much wood as a belt sander, but are far more easily controlled and leave a far smoother surface at the end. They're not much cheaper, though, when you start talking about the heavy-duty models.

Grade C plywood is of less use to the woodworker, because it's probable that even backer boards and floors of projects are best made of B-B or B-C grade plywood to save excessive filling and labor. Grade C is a rough grade, mostly useful for sheathing and, in C-plugged, for underlayment for wood floors. C-plugged has gaps filled or plugged.

B-grade panels make ideal backer board for Micarta and other plastic laminates. This unit became the top for a router table.

Grade D is a backer veneer in CDX and a filler ply in other plywoods.

Softwood plywoods are available in differing combinations of face veneers. There is N-N for clear finishing on both sides, or N-A for clear and paint, and there's also N-B for use when the back side is not visible in the finished project. In fact, you can find N-D for use when the back won't be seen or handled. Grade A comes in A-A and A-B at most suppliers, and B comes in B-B and B-C, with lesser variants available on special order (by lesser, I mean a lower-grade back veneer).

In general, you'll find softwood plywood available in 4-foot by 8-foot sheets, with 4-foot by 9-foot and 4-foot by 10-foot also easily found. For wider panels, which woodworking almost never requires (in many, many years, I've never needed a 5-foot-wide plywood panel for *anything* at all), special order is almost a certainty.

Study your needs carefully and specify the size and type of panel you want. There is no point in working with N-N when one face will be a wall panel and the other face will be turned to the wall. Too, cabinets seldom take more than one good side: Use a top grade for the outside, and a lower grade for the inside.

Hardwood Plywoods

I've already discussed the reasons for using hardwood plywoods, but it may be worth covering some ground again to stress the fact that paying a premium over solid wood can be worthwhile.

The first and foremost reason to

use hardwood plywood, as with any plywood, is the dimensional stability the laid-up plies add to any job. Layers are crossbanded (laid at 90 degrees to each other) in laid-up construction. Particleboard between veneers is also stable, and is cheaper, but is very heavy and doesn't hold screws well. Lumber core hardwood plywoods have a solid wood core with face and back veneers, and two more crossband veneers. All veneer has face and back veneers, with crossband veneers, and a veneer core. Strength is close to uniform— it is not exactly uniform—across and with the face grain because of the crossbanding.

Plywoods come in a wide variety of thickness with no need to crank up the planer: You can almost always get ⅛-inch, ¼-inch, ⅜-inch, ½-inch and ¾-inch, with ⁷⁄₁₆-inch, ⅝-inch, ⅞-inch and 1-inch often available.

I've never come to a conclusion on the advantage of the large sheets, in 4-foot by 8-foot size most of the time. It is great for storage (most of the time), but hateful to cut accurately and to move around (try particleboard core in 1-inch thickness, at about 100 or 110 pounds per panel, for a real joy on a hot summer day).

Super-grade birch furniture plywood shows *no* voids at edges or elsewhere.

Still, panels in 2 foot by 2 foot, 4 foot by 4 foot and 2 foot by 4 foot are also available, again at a slight price premium, this time over the full-sized sheet.

Color and grain matching is available in premium grades: You can do this in solid wood, but it is a distinct chore.

Almost no hardwood plywood is going to be cheaper than the solid wood you process yourself. It can't be, for all the wood in the panel must be found, cut, dried and assembled,

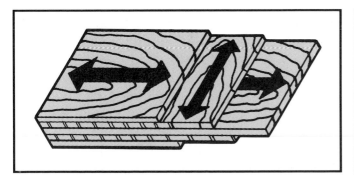

Veneer Core: The most common core type, with all inner plies made from softwood or hardwood veneer. Employs a standard cross-ply technique with three, five, seven or nine plies (including the face and back) used to produce the final panel. Structural strength and stability make veneer core panels particularly well suited to cabinet and case work.

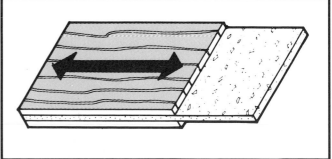

Solid Core: Solid cores consist of particleboard or medium density fiberboard (MDF). Exceptionally stable; used for applications where flatness is required.

after which it's trimmed and shipped and sold. If you're processing lumber yourself, you're buying local hardwoods, picking them up yourself, and carting them home where they dry at no cost after which you plane and joint them to your exact needs. In most cases, hardwood plywood costs a little more per square foot than does solid wood of the same species. But it is often worth it. That's a decision you must make.

American hardwood plywoods are your best bet: Baltic birch is even stronger than American, but it's also more costly. The Taiwanese, Japanese and Indonesian versions of various American hardwoods are not accurately machined to thickness. Being off $1/32$ inch doesn't seem like a lot, but the day you run a 4-foot or 8-foot dado to accept a ¾-inch-thick piece and find it off that much is the day you swear off using junk. Too, the veneers on face and back may be too thin to work properly. Most American veneers are about $1/30$ of an inch, while walnut may slip in at $1/32$, but foreign stuff may be thinner than that, which creates problems both with sawing and sanding.

You can lower the cost of hardwood plywoods if you design your project to get the most use possible out of a standard-sized (4-foot by 8-foot) panel. This may take a few tries with graph paper to see how the parts lay out, but it's worth the effort, because it also saves energy in laying out and cutting the panel when it comes time to build the project. Don't forget to leave room for the saw kerfs, about ⅛ inch minimum at each cut.

Hardwood Plywood Grades

Hardwood grades seem to depend at least in part on who you buy it from, and who makes it. Georgia-Pacific likes A, B, C and D. D is cabinet grade: allowed color streaks, color variations, mineral streaks, pin knots, small burls, some sound or filled larger knots, repaired joins, slight shakes, mixed sapwood and heartwood, and no limit on maximum number of components. In other words, it ain't much, and you should pay accordingly. Craftsman, or C, grade is better, but only by a little, so should be correspondingly priced—about a dollar a panel with most woods. Select, or B, is another story. In some woods (maple, for one) color mismatches and streaks are allowed, but otherwise, you're looking at a reasonably good wood. Grade A is a step up from there, with only slight color streaks allowed, with no shake or pin knots allowed, and it is generally a superb-looking wood.

But we need to consider uses when thinking of superb and not so superb woods. Some of the uses we have will find C a much more sensible choice than A or B.

Generally, hardwood plywood breaks down into the following choices:

• Premium: Pieces are slip or book matched unless rotary-cut one-piece is used. Small burls and pin knots, but not many, are allowed.

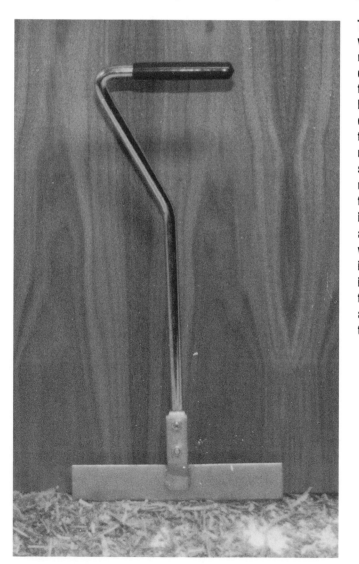

This book-matched walnut plywood is more easily handled with Leichtung's plywood handler. The handler gives an effectively longer arm reach with wide sheets of plywood, making carrying the material easier—but don't fool about outside on windy days. I used it to carry some ½-inch plywood in 15 to 20 mph winds, and felt like I was tacking a sailboat.

1. Good: Unmatched slices are allowed, but there may be no sharp contrasts in color, grain or figure. More variations are allowed, including burls, color streaks, pin knots and small patches in limited numbers.

2. Sound: No figure, color or grain match is made. Smooth patches, sound knots, discoloration and variable color are allowed.

3. Utility: Rejected material for the first three grades. Open knots, splits, wormholes to an inch long and major discoloration are all to be found.

• Shop grade has defects that knock Good or Premium panels down, in the form of factory seconds.

Note that Premium, 1, 2 and 3 pretty much correspond to Georgia-Pacific's standards of A, B, C, D. Note, too, that hardwood plywood is pretty variable stuff, and different species will be allowed different numbers and types of faults before a panel is rejected. Maple, birch and ash, for example, are allowed a lot more color variation than are lauan, cherry and mahogany.

Buying hardwood plywood is more difficult than buying softwood plywood. Most lumberyards don't stock much of a selection, but can special order it. You may have to try several times to get what you want: I wanted something more than cabinet-grade oak a while ago, and had to try several times to get it ordered, because the distributor kept claiming to be out.

Always inspect the lumber before loading, if you're hauling, or before and during unloading, if you paid for delivery.

EDGING

Covered plywood edges are a sign of a good job, whether you're using hardwood or softwood plywood. There are many ways to cover edges, some simple, some less easy.

Edge banding of hardwood plywoods is the latest "hot" method, where real wood edge banding is applied using a machine to glue it in place. The Freud I use most takes a 250-foot coil of real wood, with a glue backing. This is unfurled as the wood is moved by, placed and finally cut against the edge to be covered. The unit has a heat gun that applies heat, and pressure comes from an integral plate, so the joint is covered nicely. There are many types of banding for use with the Freud edge-banding system, including a number of woods—I keep at least birch and white oak on hand, and find walnut and cherry are also handy. You can also buy plastic edge banding for a contrast in finishes, or to match or contrast with plastic laminates.

If you don't wish to buy the edge-banding machine, use a home flat-iron: The iron is run over the front of the band, melting the glue and providing a good edge cover. The banding stores well, too: Recently, I found a white oak roll that disappeared in the shop at least five years ago. I tested it on some scrap ply-

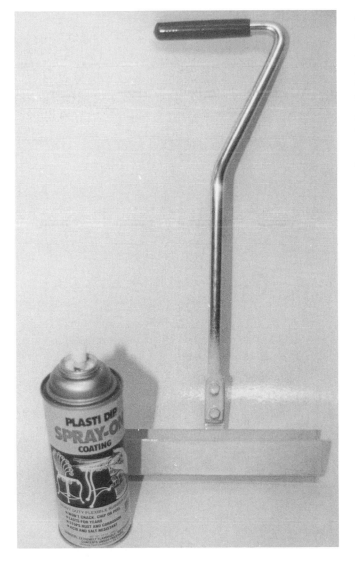

Plasti Dip's rubber spray coating works nicely to prevent scratches on expensive plywoods. Use four or more coats for the best job.

Edge-banding machines do a super job of speeding up edge-banding application—it's also more accurate than doing it by hand with a flatiron.

wood and found adhesion superb. Other types of edge banding use straight strips, with or without glue. Those without glue can be installed with any type of adhesive, including contact cement which requires no clamping. If you use regular adhesives, clamping will be needed: You may use 2-inch-wide masking tape to clamp the edge band to the structure at 12-inch intervals.

Cutting a miter on corners automatically covers raw edges. It's a simple process if your table saw comes equipped with an aftermarket fence, and you have an accurate blade angle set up. Otherwise, long miters (really, bevels) can drive you nuts. Freehand rip miters are exceptionally difficult whether done with a handsaw or a circular saw.

Solid wood edging is often really nice. It's what I used on my new desk, in part, with edge banding on the rest. Cut to just a fraction oversize for the plywood, the edging is glued in place. Contact cement is not suitable for thicker materials such as this, so yellow glue should be used.

That means clamping, best done with edge clamps: The edge clamps I'm using work very nicely for this job.

Wood filler also serves as an edge filler for plywood when the edges are to be painted. It is simple to use, fast and low cost.

You may use solid wood edging in matching or contrasting colors. Walnut looks great on maple and cherry, while maple looks fine on walnut, for example. Properly concealed plywood edges appear as attractive as solid wood.

OVERLAYS

Overlaid plywoods can serve as desktops and also provide an especially smooth finish for different paints, including enamels where finishing is much easier if the underlying surface is very smooth.

There are two types of overlay, with *Medium Density Overlay* (MDO) probably of most use to most woodworkers. The basic plywood is an Exterior grade type (with waterproof glue), and is available in Marine as well, and in B-B, with inner

plies at least C grade. The overlay is a resin treatment on fiber to provide a smooth and uniform-textured surface aimed at taking paint extremely well. For the MDO panels, overlay thickness has to be at least 0.012-inch thick.

High Density Overlay differs in that "hard" is added to the specs for the surface, so that the phenolic resin overlay is the same thickness but contains more solids than does MDO.

Special overlays are available, but woodworkers aren't going to be able to afford any such thing, as they are specially engineered for a specific purpose and usually manufactured in short runs, something that raises costs dramatically.

ORIENTED STRAND BOARD AND WAFERBOARD

Oriented strand board (OSB) and *waferboard* are two tickets on the same train. The primary difference is directional. OSB has its basis in strands of wood, reconstituted with resins to form a panel in standard panel sizes and thicknesses. Heat and pressure are used to make a tough, useful, fairly rough panel that may be produced as a single ply, or as the center laminate in composite panels, or that may be laminated in panels themselves, with no veneers. Waferboard is another nonveneered panel of wood, but made of wood wafers, again bonded under heat and pressure to form a sheet. I've not seen waferboard as a center piece of a composite panel of any kind, and don't find it referred to as such, so it just comes in plywood panel sizes, in thicknesses from ¼ inch to at least ¾ inch.

Both types of board are useful for construction of jigs around the shop, for templates, and as walls in the shop (¼-inch works nicely as a wall in shops and offices, especially with furring strips dividing it into 24-inch vertical sections for appearance). The panels take paint decently, and I've used a few of the ¼-inch as backer boards in cabinets where they serve about as well as hardboard, though they're not really useful if too visible.

TEMPERED HARDBOARD

Tempered hardboard is mostly found these days in the form of pegboard, and in various sizes as backer boards for cabinets and low-end book-shelves. It is available in most panel sizes, from 2 × 2 on up to 4 × 8 and possibly larger, but I have yet to find a way to save one dime when buying the stuff. You don't need enough to buy in bulk, and there's no other way to fiddle a price break, unless you can find edge-damaged material to suit your project sizes. And that's a theme that applies to all sheet goods: If you can find damaged material, it will be cheaper than undamaged (although I've had lumberyards try to hold me up for full price on damaged T1-11,

a type of plywood siding surface. This left me scratching my head).

VENEERS

Many of the hardwood plywoods work somewhat like their solid wood counterparts—and the lumber core types work even more like their parent woods. But there are considerable differences, both in grading and working, starting with the way the wood is cut to make face veneers.

Rotary-peeled veneer cuts are probably the most common both in hardwoods and softwoods when plywood is to be the end result. The log is mounted on a lathe and turned against an exceptionally sharp blade, peeling off a very thin veneer. The cut follows the annual growth rings, producing a very bold variegated figure, one that is fairly characteristic of softwood plywoods.

Plain or flat-sliced veneer cuts find a flitch, made of half a log (cut long ways) mounted with the heart side flat against the guide plate. The knife slices parallel to a line through the center of the log and produces a figure similar to that seen with a flat-sawn log and solid wood.

Half-round slicing uses an off-center mount for log segments (trimmed halves), cutting slightly across the annual growth rings and producing a pattern that shows modified characteristics of both rotary and flat-sliced veneers. This may be called quarter-slicing by some, and the method is often used on red and white oak to show up figures.

Rift cuts are used in oaks, and show the medullary rays we looked at much earlier to best advantage. Also called a comb cut, the cut is made perpendicular to the medullary rays, which radiate from the center of the log on out.

Veneer Matching

Veneer matching is a feature of hardwood plywood production (and one that takes place, to a slight degree, in Grade N softwood faces). There are two primary types of matching, and three other methods of veneering hardwood plywood.

Book match is made like opened pages of a book, with identical opposite patterns. The book match is made by turning over every other piece of the veneer that has been

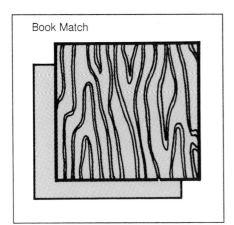

Book Match is accomplished by turning over every other piece of progressive veneer peeled from the same log. The finished face resembles the opened pages of a book, with opposite patterns identical.

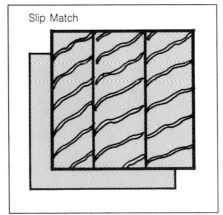

Slip Match: Progressive pieces of veneer are joined side by side, same sides up. The result is a grain pattern more uniform than Book Match.

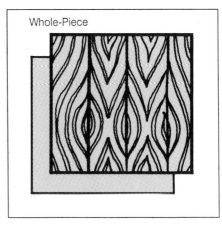

Whole-Piece uses a single piece of veneer to expose a continuous grain characteristic across the entire panel.

peeled from the same log.

Slip match is made by joining progressive pieces of veneer side by side to give a more uniform figure overall than is possible with book matching.

Whole piece veneering does what it says: A single piece of veneer exposes a figure across the entire panel.

Pleasing match means the face veneer is matched for color at the veneer joint, but not necessarily matched for figure characteristics.

Mismatch or random match occurs when veneer pieces are joined to create a casual unmatched effect. You'll see a lot of this in real veneer wall paneling.

Unmatched veneer is assembled with no attention paid to figure, color or uniformity. Such panels are usually used for project backs, and are considerably cheaper than either book or slip matches.

The last two are usually the cheapest, so if you're working up a relatively small project that needs insets of hardwood plywood that can be cut from the patterns in unmatched or mismatched veneer, jump on these types.

PRESSURE-TREATED WOOD

Most wood needs enhancing in durability for weather exposure and ground contact use. This was once largely done with creosote and similar chemicals, often by simply coating the wood with them.

Even the most attractive woods are turned downright ugly with a creosote treatment, and the chemical itself creates other problems, including severe allergic reactions for a large percentage of those exposed to it. I've watched my forearms turn red and sore a couple times, and will never do so again.

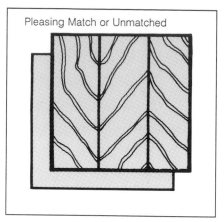

Pleasing Match: The face veneer is matched for color at the veneer joint, but not necessarily matched for grain characteristics. Unmatched is assembled with no regard for color, pattern or grain uniformity.

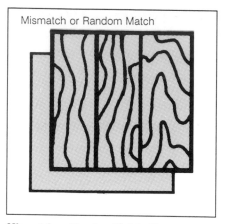

Mismatch or Random Match: Veneers are joined with the intention of creating a casual unmatched effect. Veneers from several logs may be used in the manufacture of these panels.

Modern pressure treatment of wood for home and woodshop use does not leave surface coatings of leachable materials, though it may impart a different color to the wood (usually green from the chromated copper arsenates used to treat most wood). The chemicals do not leach out of the wood, making pressure-treated wood safe for most uses that do not require contact with food (pressure-treated woods are not suitable, for example, as cutting boards or butcher-top style countertops). Thus, pressure treatment is the most common method of preparing wood for outdoor uses where durability is an essential.

Pressure-treated wood is treated with CCA (chromated copper arsenate) preservative for long-term resistance to wood-destroying organisms such as fungi and termites. For residential uses, most PT woods carry lifetime warranties.

Levels of Treatment

Pressure-treated wood receives treatment to certain specific levels, with greater treatment levels, or chemical retention rates, for wood that is in contact with the ground, or salt or brackish water. For general outdoor use, treatment to a retention level of 0.40 pounds per cubic foot is suitable for wood used both above-ground and with ground contact. The wood is dried after treatment, reducing problems with dimensional shifts and making the wood lighter and easier to handle: Check this with your local supplier. For simple outdoor use, 0.25 pounds-per-cubic-foot retention may be enough in some areas, but it does not protect in ground contact, or not very well.

Using Pressure-Treated Wood

Outdoors, near or in contact with the ground, if you don't use a naturally rot-resistant wood, then you must use one that is pressure-treated. Pressure treatment is far more effective than soaking boards in a wood preservative, and a great deal cheaper than trying to work with naturally preserved woods. Chemical preservatives to protect the wood cells from moisture and decay are forced into the wood cells under pressure. Often, spaced knifelike cuts are made into the boards to aid chemical penetration. While you don't want such cuts showing on deck planks or rails, they won't be seen in some under-deck uses.

One good reason for using pressure-treated wood instead of naturally rot-resistant wood is economic. As mentioned, pressure-treated wood is much less costly than any of the naturally resistant woods. Simply put, the major cost for such wood is for the chemicals that are shipped in long distance. Pressure treatment may be done with any of a number of locally available softwoods, thus enforcing good economy. Many hardwoods do not accept pressure treating well, and in most cases pressure treating is done on local softwoods; hardwoods are seldom treated.

Another good reason for using pressure-treated lumber is long life. The expected lifespan of properly pressure-treated woods is fifty years or more. Naturally rot-resistant woods, on the other hand, may last about ten years. To get the maximum lifespan from pressure-treated wood, soak a do-it-yourself wood preservative into the sawed off ends of the boards before installing them.

A decade ago, pressure-treated wood was available in boards and heavier lumber, such as 2×4, 2×6, 2×12, 4×4 and so on. That was it. If you wanted any fancier treatments for your deck or other projects, you had to form the wood yourself, sometimes reducing treatment effectiveness. Now, PT wood from Osmose, and other makers, is available as stair treads, stair stringers, radiused deck boards, railing tops and bottoms, spindles, turned caps, and in many other forms at moderate cost—and with far less effort required to get a unique appearance for your project, whether deck, gazebo or birdhouse. (I don't use PT wood for contact areas of birdhouses and bird feeders, but it's superb for roofs, some sides and decorative parts.) Lattice is available as well, in several weights, to provide various types of protection and screening.

Selecting Treatment Levels

Pressure-treated lumber comes in several steps of preservation, pressure-treated to a 0.25 chemical retention rate for general exposure. This is suitable for all outdoor uses except inground or ground contact. For ground contact and most general-purpose uses, you will need ground contact pressure-treated lumber, which has been treated to a 0.40 chemical retention rate. Ground contact wood is for posts, beams and joists underneath a deck.

Retention rate is the amount of chemical preservative remaining in the wood after treatment. It is stated in pounds-per-cubic-foot of wood; the higher the retention rate, the more resistance to decay. Wood used for All Weather Foundation purposes, where it is in ground contact, or below grade, is treated to 0.60, and wood for use around brackish water will be treated to 1.00 pounds-per-cubic-foot.

Where use is for foundations, or fresh water immersion, pines are treated to 0.80 pounds-per-cubic-foot and Douglas fir to 1.00 pounds-per-cubic-foot. Structural poles receive treatment leaving 0.60 pounds-per-cubic-foot in the wood.

Safety

Today's pressure-treated woods are generally safer to use than many of the older types. Nevertheless, take a few precautions. Wear gloves whenever handling pressure-treated lumber. Also, to keep sawdust and sanding dust off your skin and out of your lungs, wear gloves, tight-fitting safety goggles, and a good dust mask when sawing and sanding. Wash up immediately after work and before eating. Wash all clothing separately from other laundry. Properly dispose of scraps and sawdust from pressure-treated lumber. Do *not* burn them. Take the debris to a proper landfill or other locally recommended disposal site.

Retailers who sell pressure-treated wood offer information sheets to consumers listing all precautions to take.

Finishing Pressure-Treated Wood

Weathering of the wood surface eventually degrades even pressure-treated wood, so it needs to be finished. CCA preservatives form an excellent base for stain or paint. Water repellents, with or without topical preservatives, also make good finishes for wood that is to retain its natural look. Such repellents are now available in colors that actually closely match those of real redwood or cedar, too.

WOOD PRESERVATIVES

Make sure that all wood in contact with the ground is naturally rot-resistant or, and better, pressure-treated for ground contact use (a minimum 0.40 retention rate).

When wood is cut to fit into different parts of the project, it is best to treat the cut areas with a good quality preservative before completing nailing or screwing the parts in place.

Successful addition of wood-preserving liquids to woods, pressure treated or not, depends on how much of the preservative soaks into the wood. Brushing the preservative on is easy, but not very effective. The preservative makes a very slight surface penetration. A more effective method is to soak wood overnight. Typical penetration by soaking is four times that of a brush-on application. This still gets only 1/10- to 1/8-inch preservative penetration, which is about as much as can be expected with field treatment preservation methods. It is an improvement over brushing on, and also an indication of why pressure treatment is a far better alternative.

Cut ends cannot always be soaked, but soaking with a mop or brush is better than just brushing on, if not as effective as an overnight soak. Keep soaking until the wood refuses to accept any more preservative, then let dry and soak again.

Among the problems that may occur with wood constantly exposed to weather are decay, termites and weathering.

WOOD DECAY

Selecting the proper wood for use in outdoor projects, particularly in those parts that must be durable in contact with and under the ground, is especially important. Among other problems, decay must be prevented.

Decay in wood is caused by fungi. Control of decay requires depriving the fungi of one of the needs for their existence and growth—warmth, or moisture, or air. Wood must be damp to rot. Dry rot exists only as a name: Dry wood cannot rot, regardless of folklore. Wood with less than a 20 percent moisture content will not rot. The wood in outdoor furniture, kept off the ground, usually will not rot. Wood close to or in contact with the ground is very susceptible to rotting.

In desert areas, wood used without treatment often has a very long life. But most of us do not live in areas where the year-round humidity is under 15 percent, so some way of enhancing decay resistance is essential to durability of outdoor projects. Wood treated with chemical preservatives has increased rot (decay) resistance. Outdoor projects call for either treated wood, preferably pressure-treated, or one of the three naturally rot-resistant woods—heartwood cedar, cypress or heartwood redwood.

Weathering

There is a second possibility, beyond immediate mechanical damage, for wear and tear of wood, and that's water damage, a major part of weathering damage. Water entering the wood makes it expand and contract, creating ever-enlarging cracks that allow further penetration of water, and of termites and fungi, deep down into areas that might not be reached by treatment. Any wood in an area subject to rain, snow, sleet and so on is, of course, susceptible to weather damage. General treatment for such conditions includes the use of paints, stains, clear lacquer coatings and water repellents.

Termites

Termite damage is a problem in wide areas of the United States and Canada. The same treatment that helps prevent decay caused by fungi also keeps termites from making a series of meals of your projects.

And that's the story of wood for the woodworker, a story aimed at saving you some dollars, and helping you have a lot of fun.

We haven't covered every wood, or every way to have fun with wood as you get ready for woodworking, but we've covered the important ones. As you mature in wood selection, handling and preparation, you'll gain the hands-on knowledge that is such an important part of any kind of woodworking. Regardless of books read and desires flashed through the mind, woodworking requires application of hands to boards. Work with wood, starting with these basics, and move on to greater knowledge and enjoyment.

Do the application with appreciation, even love, of your material, and your projects will be more fun to design, work, finish, and finally, use.

CORE CONSTRUCTION

Core Type	Thickness	Advantages	Disadvantages
Veneer (all inner plies of wood veneer)	¼″ — 3 plies 5/16″ thru ½″ — 5 plies Over ½″ — 7 plies or more	Inexpensive Inexpensive; best screw-holding power	Core imperfection may telegraph through face veneers. Exposed edges may show core voids and imperfections. More susceptible to warpage.
Particleboard	¼″ thru ¾″ — 3 plies	Most stable. No core telegraphing. Generally least expensive.	Poor edge screw-holding. Heaviest core.
MDF	¼″ thru ¾″ — 3 plies	Smooth exposed edges; stable.	Heavy core.

Airstream Dust Helmets

Hwy. 54 S.
P.O. Box 975
Elbow Lake MN 56531
　(800) 328-1792
　(218) 685-4457
　(218) 685-4458 FAX

Airstream distributes the Racal line of lung and eye protection helmets—respirators—that provide protection from dust, lacquers, glues and strippers; they also distribute hearing protectors, safety glasses, and a negative (no air pump) respirator for those who don't wish to pay the cost of the positive (pumped air) systems.

American Machine & Tool Company

Fourth Ave. and Spring St.
Royersford PA 19468-2519
　(215) 948-0400
　(215) 948-5300 FAX
　(800) 435-8665 for orders
　(800) 435-3279 for customer service, parts, inquiries

American Machine & Tool Company distributes low to moderate cost tools made in Taiwan and a range of accessories.

Constantine

2050 Eastchester Rd.
Bronx NY 10461
　(800) 223-8087

Constantine's has been in business since 1812, in one form or another. Almost any aspect of woodworking, with an emphasis on veneers, is found in the full-color catalog.

Delta International Machinery Corp.

　(800) 438-2486

The line of Delta power tools includes the Unisaw table saw and the 6-inch jointer. The home shop machinery catalog offers just about anything most of us can want, or come close to affording; the industrial machinery catalog offers truly heavy-duty machinery for the huge jobs where dead-on accuracy is a must.

Garrett Wade Company

161 Avenue of the Americas
New York NY 10013-1299
　(800) 221-2942

The lush regular catalog shows a wide variety of hand tools and power tool accessories, including the widest array of chisels of any company.

Groff & Hearne Lumber

858 Scotland Rd.
Quarryville PA 17566
　(800) 342-0001
　(717) 284-0001

Groff & Hearne supplies curly cherry and many other fine woods up to 40 inches wide, with specialization in walnut and cherry. Lumber is sold rough or dressed, there is no minimum order, and orders may be shipped UPS or common carrier (truck).

Leichtung Workshops

4944 Commerce Pkwy.
Cleveland OH 44128
　(800) 237-5907
　(216) 464-6764

Leichtung offers a variety of unusual tools, some woodworking supplies and a free catalog featuring joint-making jigs, some kits (varying with the seasons, but often small boxes and clocks), router bits, Lervad folding workbenches, and a multitude of small items.

Lignomat USA Ltd.

P.O. Box 30145
Portland OR 92301
　(800) 227-2105
　(503) 257-8957

Lignomat moisture meters are probably the best-known of all such units. A free brochure explains one or more of the many models they produce, with an array starting at the pocket-sized Mini-Lignometer, the Ligno-master K100 and the G1000. There is an in-kiln model, too, and a newly introduced Thermo-hygrometer for shops and other wood storage areas.

McFeely's

P.O. Box 3
Lynchburg VA 24505
　(800) 443-7937
　(804) 847-7136 FAX

If you want instruction in square drive screws, the McFeely's catalog is the place to get it. Pages are devoted to telling you everything from the reasons for using square drive screws, to screw size needs for particular types of work, and on to screw head styles and lengths to use.

Miracle Point

P.O. Box 71
Crystal Lake IL 60014-0071
　(815) 477-7713

Miracle Point has one product line, tweezers, and at a reasonable cost there is a version that specifically suits woodworkers, so no catalog is sent.

Bob Morgan Woodworking Supplies, Inc.

1123 Bardstown Rd.
Louisville KY 40204
(502) 456-2545
(502) 456-4752 FAX

Bob Morgan emphasizes veneers in his catalog, but also sells a variety of solid hardwoods, domestic and imported. Morgan is noted for packaging cut-offs at low prices, and now sells ebony mill ends among such packages. Small tools and hardware are spotted throughout the catalog as well.

Ryobi American Corp.

1424 Pearman Diary Rd.
Anderson SC 29625
(800) 323-4615

Ryobi makes a wide variety of products, from printing equipment through lawn and garden products to hardware and sporting goods, but probably the most relevant other line is a die casting company that has helped them produce top grade lightweight aluminum castings for most of their tools. Ryobi also makes benchtop tools and portable power tools.

Trend-Lines

375 Beacham St.
Chelsea MA 02150
(800) 366-6966 Catalog request number

Trend-Lines is a discount mail order house, and a distributor of its own Reliant line of power tools including planers and jointers.

UGL (United Gilsonite Laboratories)

P.O. Box 70
Scranton PA 18501
(800) UGL-LABS

Manufacturers of ZAR wood finishing products, including penetrating wood stains, clear polyurethane varnishes in gloss, satin and flat finishes, and exterior polys in brush-on and spray formulations. Also ZAR Aqua, a new line of clear polyurethanes that are water-based, thereby cutting odors, flammability dangers and solvent emissions problems.

Williams & Hussey Machine Co., Inc.

Riverview Mill
P.O. Box 1149
Wilton NH 03086
(800) 258-1380
(603) 654-6828
(603) 654-5446 FAX

The W&H molder-planer unit offers quick blade changes and a capacity of almost double blade width because one side is open, allowing double pass cutting. The unit also takes moulding cutting blades, to double utility.

Wood-Mizer Products, Inc.

8180 W. Tenth St.
Indianapolis IN 46214
(317) 271-1542
(800) 553-0182

Wood-Mizer sells portable band saw sawmills. There are several versions (six), and the catalog then goes on to describe Solar Dry kilns to finish up the work.

Woodcraft

210 Wood County Industrial Park
P.O. Box 1686
Parkersburg WV 26102-1686
(800) 225-1153
(800) 535-4482 for customer service
(800) 535-4486 for technical advice

Woodcraft's catalog is second in attractiveness to Garrett Wade's only because the photography is a touch less lush, slanting more to information presentation in top-grade photographs, without exotic lighting. It is just as colorful, just as well photographed, and there are many unusual items.

Woodworkers' Store

21801 Industrial Blvd.
Rogers MN 55374-9514
(612) 428-2199
(612) 428-8668 FAX

Another major mail order source for many items, The Woodworkers' Store carries a wide line of tools, woods, finishes, plans, jigs, kits, and a very wide line of hardware, including many porcelain parts, oak and birch carvings. They also supply baltic birch and hardwood plywood and turning blanks of ebony and kingwood.

Woodworker's Supply

5604 Alameda Pl. NE
Albuquerque NM 87113
(800) 645-9292
(505) 821-0578

Not only does Woodworker's Supply offer a wide variety of tools and project supplies, it offers stores in Casper, Wyoming (307-237-5528), and Graham, North Carolina (919-578-0500). They offer Woodtek stationary tools in addition to the standard lines from Delta and other makers.

INDEX

More Great Books for Woodworkers!

How to Sharpen Every Blade in Your Woodshop — You know that tools perform best when razor sharp—yet you avoid the dreaded chore. This ingenious guide brings you plans for jigs and devices that make sharpening any blade quick and simple! Includes jigs for sharpening chisels, boring & drilling bits, router bits and more! #70250/$17.99/144 pages/157 b&w illus./paperback

Make Your Own Jigs & Woodshop Furniture — Innovative jigs and fixtures will help you specialize your ordinary power tools without spending big money. You'll get plans for over 40 jigs and fixtures, 23 projects for a well-outfitted workshop and more! #70249/$24.99/144 pages/200 illus./paperback

Creating Your Own Woodshop — Discover dozens of economical ways to fill unused space with the woodshop of your dreams. Charles Self shows you how to convert space, layout the ideal woodshop, or improve your existing shop. #70229/$18.95/128 pages/162 illus./paperback

Building Fine Furniture from Solid Wood — You'll build beautiful wood furniture with 11 of Sadler's most popular projects complete with instructions, exploded drawings, and detailed photographs. #70230/$24.95/160 pages/210 illus.

The Woodworker's Sourcebook — Shop for woodworking supplies from home! Self has compiled listings for everything from books and videos to plans and associations. Each listing has an address and telephone number and is rated in terms of quality and price. #70208/$19.99/160 pages/200 photos

Measure Twice, Cut Once — Achieve good proportion, clean cuts, and snug fits every time! You'll learn what each measuring tool does, how to use it properly—even how to make your own. #70210/$18.95/128 pages/143 illus./paperback

Building & Restoring the Hewn Log House — If you yearn for the rustic life, this practical guide will help you build or restore the traditional log cabin. #70228/$18.95/176 pages/265 illus./paperback

The Complete Guide to Restoring and Maintaining Wood Furniture and Cabinets — Don't let nicks, scratches and dozens of other imperfections ruin your treasured heirlooms. Detailed instructions show you how to repair damage and restore gorgeous finishes. #70209/$19.95/160 pages/paperback

Basic Woodturning Techniques — Detailed explanations of fundamental techniques like faceplate and spindle turning will have you turning beautiful pieces in no time. #70211/$14.95/112 pages/119 illus./paperback

Good Wood Handbook — Your guide to selecting and using the right wood for the job (before you buy). You'll see a wide selection of commercial softwood and hardwoods in full color. #70162/$16.95/128 pages/250+ color illus.

Blizzard's Book of Woodworking — Step-by-step demonstrations for a wide range of projects for home and garden will hone your skills and improve your technique. #70163/$22.95/208 pages/350+ illus.

Pocket Guide to Wood Finishes — This handy guide gives you instant visual guidance for mixing stains and other finishes. Spiral bound and durable—perfect for your woodshop. #70164/$16.95/64 pages/200+ color illus.

The Art of Fine Furniture Building — Twenty projects with fully illustrated plans and price lists show you how to create professional quality furniture on a budget. #70195/$16.95/176 pages/110 photos/illus./paperback

Make Your Woodworking Pay for Itself — Find simple hints for selling your work to pay for shop improvements or generate a little extra income! #10323/$16.95/128 pages/30 illus./paperback

Gary Branson's Home Repairs and Improvements on a Budget — Save money with step-by-step instructions that show you how to quiet floor noises, prevent drain clogs, locate wall studs, and hundreds of other easy do-it-yourself projects! #70247/$16.99/160 pages/128 illus./paperback

Rehab Your Way to Riches — Let a real estate mogul show you how to generate real estate income in ways that limit risk and maximize profits. #70156/$14.95/208 pages/paperback

The Complete Guide to Being Your Own Remodeling Contractor — This helpful guide will ensure that remodeling jobs get done right! Checklists will help you spot work that's not up to snuff, plus you'll control your costs with handy material lists. #70246/$18.99/288 pages/150 illus.

The Complete Guide to Contracting Your Home — Vital information on financing your home, choosing a site, and working with suppliers and inspectors all in one handy book! #70025/$18.99/288 pages/paperback

The Complete Guide to Four-Season Home Maintenance — With some simple tips and techniques, you'll minimize costly repairs and replacements—all year round! #70192/$18.95/160 pages/92 illus./paperback

The Complete Guide to Residential Deck Construction — Everybody loves an outdoor deck! Find all the information you need to plan, design and construct a deck whether you're doing it by yourself or with the help of a contractor. #70035/$16.95/176 pages/50 photos/illus./paperback

The Complete Guide to Remodeling Your Basement — Whether you need a special place for your workshop, more family space, or just want to increase the value of your home, you'll find all you need to start and finish the job in these pages. #70034/$14.95/176 pages/50 photos/illus./paperback

Home Improvements: Making Investments in Your Home That Pay for Themselves — You'll discover how to evaluate improvements to get the most from your investment (without sinking a lot of money into it)! #70207/$16.95/160 pages/paperback

The Complete Guide to Building and Outfitting an Office in Your Home — You'll discover how to convert basements and attics, determine space needs, create layouts—even specifics like how to keep house sounds out! #70244/$18.99/176 pages/105 b&w illus./paperback